Feed My Lambs

Lectures to Children
On Matters of Life and Death

John Todd

Solid Ground Christian Books
Birmingham, Alabama, USA

Solid Ground Christian Books
2090 Columbiana Road
Suite 2000
Birmingham, AL 35216
(205) 443-0311
sgcb@charter.net
http://solid-ground-books.com

Feed My Lambs:
Lectures to Children on Matters of Life and Death
by John Todd (1800-1873)

New Solid Ground Classic Reprints edition April 2005

Taken from the 1857 edition by Hopkins, Bridgman and Co., Northampton

New cover design by Borgo Design, Tuscaloosa, Alabama. Contact them by
e-mail at nelbrown@comcast.net.

ISBN: 1-932474-73-0

Feed My Lambs

Author's Original Preface

In "rightly dividing the word,"[1] it is a difficult question to decide how and in what manner we can best meet the spirit of the command, "Feed my Lambs."[2] That children are a very important class in every congregation, all admit; that ministers owe them some peculiar duties is equally plain; and that they are a difficult part of the flock to feed, the experience of every one, who has ever tried to do his duty to them, will testify. Says a profound thinker, and one of uncommon knowledge of human nature,[3] "Nothing is easier than to *talk* to children; but to talk to them as they ought to be talked to, is the very last effort of ability. A man must have a vigorous imagination. He must have extensive knowledge, to call in illustration from the four corners of the earth; for he will make but little progress, but by illustration. It requires great genius, to throw the mind into the habits of children's minds. I aim at this, but I find it the utmost effort of ability. No sermon ever put my mind half so much on the stretch. I am surprised at nothing which Dr. Watts[4] did, but his Hymns for children. Other men could have written as well as he, in his other works; but how he wrote these hymns, I know not." Happy that minister who can rightly divide the word of God to this portion of his flock. Should such a one take up this little volume, he will be very ready to excuse its defects, knowing how difficult it is to bring thought down to the comprehension of children.

"It is an easy thing to move the passions: a rude, blunt, illiterate attack may do this. But to form one new figure for the conveyance of the truth to the mind is a difficult thing. The world is under no small obligation to the man who forms such a figure."

The *best* way of preaching to children is to have them *entirely* alone–not an adult in the house. You can then come down to them, and can interest them. The next best way is to have all the children in the centre of the house, and the congregation above and around them; and

---

[1] 2 Timothy 2:15.
[2] John 21:15.
[3] Richard Cecil (1748-1810) was a prominent minister in the Anglican Church and close friend of John Newton, Thomas Scott and Charles Simeon.
[4] Isaac Watts (1674-1748) was considered by many the greatest hymn-writer of all time. His Hymns have been republished by Soli Deo Gloria.

then let the speaker *forget*, if he can, that anybody is present besides the children. This has been my method, at the close of the second service on the Sabbath. The adults of the congregation have had permission to retire, but have, to an individual, preferred to remain.

I have usually delivered one of my "little Sermons" once in three months, supposing this to be no more, certainly, than the share of the lambs. The following Lectures are a selection from such as I have thus delivered to the children under my care. My language and illustrations may seem familiar and common-place; but I have tried to talk in such a manner, that, on pausing several times, and asking my little bright audience what point had just been stated and illustrated, the child who could only lisp should usually be able to throw his voice in with the rest in answering.

I have thought that a System of Theology, embracing all that we usually mean by the term, and containing a full, clear and condensed view of the doctrines of the Bible, might be prepared for children to great advantage. Nor am I certain that such a series of volumes might not be as useful and as interesting to common readers as to children. It ought to be a Text-book of the great Doctrines of the Bible, for Sabbath Schools and the young generally. That I have thought of preparing such a work, is saying little, since I have not done it. Possibly, should Providence spare my life, and such a work be needed, I may, hereafter, attempt it.[5]

I have hoped that Parents and Sabbath School Teachers might receive some hints from this little volume which would aid them in the very difficult work of illustrating truth to children. For no teaching will do any good, unless so plain that it cannot be misunderstood, and so interesting that it cannot be forgotten.

To the blessing of the Great Redeemer, I commend this little book, and the dear children who may read it.

John Todd
Northampton, MA, May 20, 1834.

Note. –The unexpected fact, that the Publisher requests a revised copy for a new edition, in less than three weeks after the first edition was out, encourages the Author to hope that he has not misjudged as to the usefulness of this little work.

June 7, 1834.

---

[5] Dr. Todd actually commenced this project five years later when he wrote and published *Truth Made Simple: Lectures to Children on the Character of God.* Solid Ground hopes to reprint this excellent volume in the summer of 2005.

2

Author's Preface to the Revised Edition

This little work, after having passed through fifteen editions in this country (USA), and we know not how many in England, after having been translated into French, German, Bulgarian, Tamil, Travancore, Greek, and many more languages, printed in raised letters for the blind, and last of all, having been adopted as a school-book for the liberated slaves at Sierra Leone, is now sent forth by the publishers in a new dress, with the addition of two new Lectures.[6] The only reason why the number was not much larger is that we wish to keep it a little book for little folks.

A whole generation has passed from childhood into manhood since these Lectures were first printed; and though it claims to be only a very humble instrument of usefulness, yet the author, from testimony which he has already received from many and various quarters, would rather want renown and fame among men, than to be without his hope that the mission of this little work has been one of good to the lambs of Christ's flock.

John Todd
Pittsfield, MA, October 1, 1852

---

[6] The additional lectures that were added to the original work are the first and the last. Todd rightly felt it wise to include the introductory lecture to reveal the four-fold goal he had in view in the book. The concluding chapter on Heaven is a fitting conclusion to this brilliant work.

3

TABLE OF CONTENTS

5

7

LECTURE I

INRODUCTORY LECTURE

"Feed my lambs." – John 21:15

Party in the grove. Food cut fine. What will be done? Bad apple. Indian book. Twenty stags. Four goals of these lectures. Learn to read the best books. Learn to think right. Mind always thinking. Ask questions. Learn to feel right. Two men in the Temple. Weeds in the garden. White rabbit. Is it sundown? Learn to do right. The regulator. What a little boy may be. The fairy and the diamond. A gem in the Savior's crown. The rose transplanted. Children's draw. More hereafter.

Children, suppose now that we and a great many more children were met in a beautiful grove on a bright, summer day. For some hours we ramble over the hills and climb the rocks, pluck the flowers around us and listen to the singing of the birds. We then come together in a very shady spot, where there is a cool spring of pure water. Here we find a long table spread and loaded with all manner of good things to eat. Suppose, too, that I am the only grown-up person with all these children, and that I am wishing to see that they all have a good share of the things to eat. Should I do wrong, or do right, to go round and cut the bread and the meat for each child, and cut it *so fine* that each one could eat with comfort? "Right," you say, I should do right, and I ought to cut the meat very fine so that all might have a share. Well, then, when I come to feed the *minds* of children, instead of their mouths, ought I not to cut the food very fine? I mean, ought I not to speak very plain, and to use such words as each child can understand? "Yes," you say, "you should be very plain and easy to be understood." This, then, is the reason why I shall

9

talk so plain, that every child, even that very little girl who has but just learned to read, can know what I mean.

You know, children, that when you see a man very busy with his tools, you think he is making something. You may not be able to see what it is, but the timber, and the chips cut off, and the tools about, and the man at hard work, all show you that he wishes to make something. So if you had seen me when I took the sheet of paper out of my drawer, and began to write this little book of Lectures, you would have supposed I had something which I wish to bring about. And so I have. There are *four* things I wish to do by these Lectures,—all for your good, and all which will be done, *if* you will help me. Let me talk a few minutes about each of these four things.

1. *I wish to make you love to read.* Cattle, birds, and dogs cannot read. They have good eyes, and good ears, and good mouths and tongues, and yet they cannot read. Not so the child. He is created in the image and likeness of God, and no wonder he can read. But you might go through an orchard that had a hundred trees in it, and yet not find more than a single tree that bore good fruit. So you might see a whole book-case filled with books, and not more than one or two good books among them all. But a bad book is not like a bad apple. The bad apple tastes bad the moment you bite it; but a bad book, like some poisonous fruits, may be pleasant while you eat it, but hurts you afterwards.

How many pure and beautiful things may we read in a single little book! A small box may contain a great many choice jewels! For my part, when a child, and ever since, I have loved to meet a book, and always feel that I have met a friend. Once, when in the deep wilderness, I was on a river in a little boat. It was very far from anybody. When we came to a place where the river was full of rocks, and where the water ran and dashed against the rocks, we knew we must carry the boat round through the

10

woods. Here we found a blind little path, where the Indians used to carry their canoes. We found that many years ago they had written a small book, containing a history of their travels and hunting, and left it here! And what kind of a book do you suppose it was? It was a part of a cedar tree hewn off, and then on the standing tree, with a piece of charcoal, they had made a picture of a canoe, with her front pointed *down* the river, to show which way they went. In the canoe was the picture of two Indians, each with a paddle in his hand, and a dog between them; then below was a picture of a deer's head with great branching horns, to show that they had been hunting deer, and the number 20, to show that they had killed twenty bucks or stags in their hunt.

This was the Indian book. But how little did it teach us! It showed that some time, a long time ago, two Indians had passed that way with their dog, and that in their hunt they had killed twenty stags. But it told us not who they were, where they had been, where going, or any valuable information. In a wilderness it was pleasant to read even such a poor book as that, but how much better to have good printed books full of good reading! Learn to love to read when a child and you will have pleasures all the way through life. You will never find a rainy day tedious, nor a journey lonely, nor even a sick bed wearisome, if you can read. Books contain the best thoughts that men ever had, and when we open them, though the authors may be dead, yet we seem to hear their voices coming to us kind and pleasant, like far-off music at evening twilight.

2. *I wish to teach you to THINK right.* Children, have you never found a boy or a girl alone, talking to himself, or herself? And if you have, did you not notice that they stopped and were ashamed when discovered? The reason was that they were talking out their thoughts just as they rose up in the mind, and they knew these thoughts were foolish. If they had been repeating over the Ten Commandments, or even the multiplication table, they would not have felt ashamed. Now the mind of every child is always thinking; but the thoughts are not of any value,—they do not think to any good purpose. What I wish is, to teach you to think that which is of some use. You know a garden will bear weeds in great plenty, if we are not careful. It will soon all run to waste, if left to itself. So the mind will run to waste if not taught to think right. This is the reason why I ask you questions, and explain things, perhaps tell you little stories, and make comparisons,—so that you may learn to think right.

If a man thinks wrong about God, or the Bible, he will do wrong. If he thinks that God cares not what a man thinks, or feels, or says, or does, he will not care himself. If he thinks that the Bible can teach him nothing good, he will not read it. If he thinks he may be selfish and live only for himself, he will be likely to do so. Or if a man learns to let his thoughts run loose like a horse without bridle or halter, like the horse they will be of no use. I want you to be able to think quick, and hard, and correctly. Then you will not only understand such books as you read, but will enjoy them, and relish them the more if they contain a great deal to make you think. A boy sometimes goes away from home, and visits a factory, or a ship, or a coal-mine, or some such thing. He sees many new things. He remembers them all, and goes home and talks about them and asks questions about them. Just so I want you should learn to notice the new thoughts you find in this little book, and then that you talk them over, and ask questions about them till you understand them fully. Will you try to do it?

3. I want to teach you to FEEL right. Did you ever read a little story which Christ told of two men who went up to the great Temple at Jerusalem to pray? The story is very beautiful.[7] One of them felt that he was good, and that he had nothing to do but to thank God that he was so much better than other people. "God," says he, "I thank thee that I am not as other men!" The other man felt that he was a poor, sinful creature. So he looked on the ground, and never lifted up his eyes, and struck his breast, and stood away off in a corner and said, "God be merciful to me a sinner." Now these men both felt,—but one felt right and the other wrong, and God looked upon them very differently. He blessed the humble man, and let the other go away in his pride and folly. So he always does.

You know, children, that if a man neglects his garden, and does not sow good seed and take care of it, the garden will shortly be covered with weeds. Weeds grow naturally, but vines and good roots do not. Just so will wrong feelings come in and grow up in the heart of a child, unless he takes pains to feel right. You must know when you feel right, and when you feel wrong. Perhaps you think you cannot tell. But let us see. Suppose a child

---

[7] See Luke 18:9-14.

13

is unwilling to obey his parents, and frets when told to do anything, and either does not do it, or goes murmuring,—does he feel right or wrong? Suppose he wants what his parents feel will not be good for him, or what they cannot afford to buy, and then he cries and frets,—does he feel right or wrong? Suppose a little boy sees another boy have a toy, or a white rabbit, and he wishes he had it, and wishes he could steal it and have nobody know it,—does he feel right or wrong? A little boy once was told that he must not play because it was the Sabbath. He asked, When will the Sabbath end? He was told, not till the sun was down. Then he thought, he wished the sun was down and the Sabbath gone, and he wished that God would not make any Sabbath, and he wished that he could go out and play and nobody know it,—did he feel right or wrong?

Now I want you to feel right at all times, in all places, and on all subjects. The reasons are three;—first, it will make you very happy; secondly, it will make others very happy; and, thirdly, it will please God. Are not these reasons plain ones and good ones?

4. *I wish to have you DO right.* Did you ever see the inside of a watch, children? Well, there are wheels and little posts, and the like, and, among other things, there is a little fine spring, so small that it looks like a hair curled up. This little spring is called the regulator, because it regulates the watch. If it be drawn too tight, the watch goes too slow. If it be too loose, the watch goes too fast. It must be just right. The regulator must be regulated. And there is in each of you something that does the work of that little spring. It is called the *conscience;* that which tells us when we do right and when we do wrong. The conscience is the regulator. But how shall we know when that is right? I reply, by the Bible; that will always tell us whether our conscience is too tight or too loose. A good book, like the Bible, will help

you to have your conscience regulated and right; and then you will act right, and do right.

I have seen little boys at work in the corn-field, or in the garden, or at school. I could not tell what they would become, or what they would do, in later life. But I have known some of them to grow up to be good and valuable farmers, some mechanics, some physicians, and some of them ministers of the Gospel. When I see a child, I never know what he will become; but I know that he *may* become an angel in God's kingdom for ever, if he will be good and do good, and trust in God. And though I may not know the child that reads this little hook,—perhaps shall never see him in this world,—yet I hope I shall hereafter see him in God's holy kingdom, with a crown of life on his head and a harp of gold in his hand.

I have somewhere read the story of a fairy to whom was given a rough-looking stone to polish. She went to work and turned it over and over, and rubbed it and polished it, till it began to be smooth, then to be bright, and then to sparkle like fire, till at last from the rough stone she polished and brought out a diamond such as would delight any king to wear in his crown. Had any one seen the fairy when she first began, he might have thought she was doing a useless and a foolish thing; but who would not like to own such a gem after it is once polished? The little child is like that rough stone. It might seem to some that it is of little consequence whether he has any books, or what books they are; but I know that every child may become like a polished diamond in the crown of the Lord Jesus Christ,—to be beautiful and glorious for ever. If I can do anything towards polishing such a gem, ought I not to be anxious to do it? And if I may do any part of this work by these Lectures, shall I not have reason to rejoice for ever? These gems are to be among the glory of Jesus Christ in the day when he is crowned.

"A babe into existence came,
A feeble, helpless, suffering frame;
It breathed below a little while,
Then vanished like a tear, a smile,
That springs and falls, that peers and parts,
The joy, the grief, of loving hearts.
The grave received the body dead,
Where all that live must lay their head.
Sank then the soul to dust and gloom,
Worms and corruption, in the tomb?
No! in 'the rainbow round the throne,'[8]
Caught up to paradise, it shone,
And still it shines, until the day
When heaven and earth shall pass away,
And those that sleep in Jesus here
With him in glory shall appear;
Then will that soul and body meet,
And, when his jewels are complete,
'Midst countless millions, form a gem
In the Redeemer's diadem!"

In the Bible, the fairest who die are called flowers; and I have often looked into the coffin of the fair and beautiful child, and thought of imagery. I have often thought that Christ sometimes treats the little child as a gardener would a rose. The little, beautiful rose hangs on its frail stem on the hillside. The storm has beaten it down into the dirt, and it is soiled and injured. The gardener takes hold of it, shakes off the dust, and then pulls it up and transplants it into his garden, where he can nurse it, and shelter it, and cause it to grow and bloom. Thus heaven is called Paradise[9] in the Bible,—as if it were a most beautiful garden,—where undying flowers shall blossom for ever. And thus Christ often seems to say to the beautiful little child, "Poor one! the storms and the frosts and winds are too rough for thee here,—and so I will take thee up and place thee in my own garden above, where thou mayest live and bloom for ever and ever!"

---

[8] Revelation 4:3.
[9] Luke 23:43; 2 Corinthians 12:4; Revelation 2:7.

Shall I not, then, try to do what I can to make these flowers worthy the notice and the love of the great Redeemer?

Sometimes, when I have done my day's work, I look into a particular drawer in which I keep such papers as I have begun to write something on to be printed; and when I see a paper on which I have begun to write for children, I say to myself, "See there! I have not written a word for children for a long time. Perhaps, if I should write, there is some little boy or some little girl, it may be far away among the mountains, or on the smooth prairie of the West, or in the crowded city,—some bright little child,—who would read what I should write, and thus I might speak to him though far away, and though I shall never see him! And perhaps what I shall say would be read and thought of when I am dead and gone, and thus I may be doing good for a long time to come!" And then I shut the drawer and feel sorry that I have done no more for my little readers, and say to myself, "I will do more hereafter!" And I pray that I may not only do so, but that I may so write that I shall meet many of my little friends in heaven, and with them praise the Savior for ever and ever! Amen.

LECTURE II

HOW DO WE KNOW THERE IS ANY GOD?

"No man hath seen God at any time." – John 1:18

Why God called by this name. Paris and London. Did anybody ever see God? The wind and trees. Anybody ever see pain? Hunger. Love. Eyes put out and ears deaf. A child can think without eyes and ears. The watch in the case. Proof of God. The meeting-house. What the meeting-house made for. A meeting-house built by chance! The silkworm. The dead rabbit and birds. The cow and horse seeing a painting. The mind is glad. The body is a house for the soul. The new book. God made things. The rainbow, flowers, and fruits, made by God. God seen plainly. When ought a child to think of God? The sincere wish.

Children have heard a great deal said about God. Our forefathers, a great while ago, used to call him *"the Good."* We shorten the word a little, and call him GOD; but it means the same thing,–*good.* And they gave him that name because he is so good to men. But I am going to ask these children a question. How do you know there is any God? Have you ever seen him? No; for "no man hath seen God at any time."

Are we sure there are things in the world which we never saw? Yes, a great many. You never saw Paris, or London, and yet you know there are such places. How do you know? You know because others have been there and *seen* them.

Now, suppose nobody had ever seen those cities, could you know there were such cities? No. How, then, do you know there is any God? Is it because the men who wrote the Bible *say* there is a God? But how do they know? They never

18

saw God. Can we believe there is anything which nobody ever saw? Yes, a great many things.

Go to the window some cold day. Do you see the trees rocking, and the limbs swinging and bending, and the leaves all flying about? What makes them do so? Can any of you tell? Yes, you all know, it is the *wind* blowing the trees. But can you see the wind? No, but every body knows there is such a thing as the wind, though we cannot see it.

Did you ever feel sick, so as to take medicine, and feel in great pain? Yes. I suppose you all have. But which of these children ever *saw* the pain? Did you hear it? No. Did you smell it? No. And you know there is such a thing as pain, though we cannot see it.

You all know there is such a thing as hunger. How do you know? You never saw it, nor heard it, nor smelt it; but you felt it.

Suppose I should now say there is no such thing in the world as love. Would it be true? No. But why not? You never saw love. No, but you love your parents, and know by your feelings that there is such a thing as love, though you never saw it.

Suppose one of these children should have both of his eyes put out, and be a blind little boy. He could still think. He could sit down and think how his home looked, how his father and mother looked. Suppose he should then lose his hearing so as to be deaf. He could still think how the voice of his father and mother used to sound, when they spoke pleasantly to him. Suppose he were then to lose his taste, so that he could not taste sweet things from sour. He could then sit down and think how food and fruit used to taste, and how he used to love them. Suppose, next, he were to lose his feeling, so as to be numb and cold. He could then think how things used to feel; how an orange felt round, and a book felt flat.

19

Yes, and if he were to lose eyes, and ears, and taste, and feeling, and smelling, all at once, he could still tell us how things used to be. The sun used to look bright and round, and so did the moon; the rose and the pink used to smell sweetly, the flute to sound pleasantly, the honey to taste sweet, and the ice to feel cold. He could think all about these things.

Now, what is it that *thinks?* It is the soul,—the soul within you. How do you know that a watch-case has any watch in it? Because you hear it tick, and see the pointers move. And just so you know your body has a soul in it, because it thinks, and moves your hand, and your eye, just as the watch within the case moves the pointers. But nobody ever saw the soul. And yet we know we have a soul, *because we see it do things.* When you feel happy, the soul makes the face laugh; when the soul feels bad, it shows itself through the face, and perhaps makes the face cry. When you feel wicked, it makes you cross, and speak wicked words, and disobey your parents, and disobey God.

Now, it is in just such ways we know there is a God. Just attend to what I am going to say, and see if I do not make it plain, and prove it all out to you, that there is a God, because *we see that he does things.*

You see this meeting-house. You see it is full of things which were planned out, and everything in it planned for some use. Now, look. This pulpit with its stairs, and window, and seat for what are they designed? Why, the window is to let the light in, the seat for the preacher to sit down, and the stairs so that he can get into it; and this place where I stand, that he may stand up so high as to be seen by all in the house. Those seats or pews were made for you to sit in, during the sermon, and all done off and numbered, so that each family might have their own pew, and know it. Those windows were made to let the light in; those posts to hold up the gallery, so that it might not fall on those who sit under it.

Those doors are made to shut the noise and the cold out, and those stoves to warm the house in winter, and the long pipes to carry off the smoke. That front gallery is for the singers to sit in and sing God's praises. Look now, and see if you can find anything to play with. No. There is nothing. Of course, this house was not made to play in. See if you can see anything to sleep on—any couch, or bed? No, none. Of course, this house was not made to sleep in. It is all planned to be a place in which to worship God.

Suppose, now, I should tell you this house was never built by anybody! It all grew up by chance, just as it is! The brick for the walls on the outside, and the roof on the top, grew just so, making this great square room, with its pews, and pulpit, and windows, and stoves, and everything just as it is! It all grew so by chance! Could you believe this? No, you could not believe it. Why, you would say, this house must be built by somebody. True. True. But tell me, did you ever see the man who made these bricks, and spread these walls? No. Did you see the carpenter who built these pews, and pulpit, and doors, and windows? No. Did you ever see the glass-maker who melted the sand and made this glass? No. Did you ever see the silk-weaver who wove this pulpit-curtain? No. Or the man who hammered out the iron and made those pipes? No, no. You never did, and yet you know that all these lived, because you see what they have done. And this is good proof.

And it is in just such ways that we know there is a God; for he made the clay, which had only to be altered by the fire, and it is brick. He made the wood, which has only to be altered in its shape, and it becomes pews and seats. He made the iron, which had only to have its shape altered by melting, and it is these stoves. The sand which he made has only to be melted, and it becomes glass. He made the little worm which spun the silk of which this cushion was made. And he made the light to shine through these windows, and your eyes to see it after it comes in, and your ears to hear voices and sounds. He made that mind of yours, so that it can understand what I say, and your memory so that you can lay it up and keep it, and talk it over after you go home.

I once saw a painting of a dead rabbit and some large birds. They looked just as if they were a real rabbit and real birds; and a little dog, coming in, jumped up to catch them in his mouth, thinking they were real. Now, could any one doubt but a painter had been there, who made that picture? No. Nor could any one doubt but there is a God, who made the rabbit and the birds.

A painter once painted a large sheaf of wheat for a baker's sign. A cow came up, and mistook it for a real sheaf, and tried to eat it. And another painter painted a horse which looked so natural, that another horse came up, and neighed to it, thinking it was a real horse. Suppose you had seen these pictures, and nobody near them; would you not at once say, "Somebody must have made those pictures?" Yes; and when you see the wheat in the field, and the horse in the street, you know that somebody made them; and that somebody is God.

Why do you love to hear a new and curious story? Is the ear pleased? No. The ear feels no pleasure. Why do you love to see something that is new, and curious, and strange? Is your eye made glad? No. The eye knows nothing about it. But your *mind* feels glad, when you hear a pleasant story, or sweet music, and when you see a new sight. The mind is glad. But how came that curious mind within you? Did it come there by chance? No, no more than this house came here by chance. The body is the house. The soul lives in it; and God has made the ear to let sounds into the soul; and the eye, so that light may go in as through a window; and the tongue, so that the soul may speak out and tell its feelings; and the feet to carry it about anywhere; and the hands to be servants, and do anything the soul wants done. And then the body needs food, and God has made it, the fire to cook it, and the teeth to chew it. It needs drink, and so he has made water, and the cow to give milk. It gets sick, and so he has made medicines to cure it. It needs clothes, and so he has made the cotton grow out of the ground, the leather on the ox, the wool on the back of the sheep, and the worm to spin the silk. It needs tools, and so he has made the iron and lead, the silver and the gold, and the wood. It needs to be warm, and so he has made and hung up the sun like a great fire to pour down his light and heat. The world is full of what God has done. Can you not see his doings everywhere?

You see this little book in my hand. It is full of pages, and maps, and printing. It is a New Testament. Here are the chapters and verses all marked out plainly and correctly. Every word and every letter is right. Now, you never saw the man, who made this paper, nor the man who put up these types, nor the man who pressed the paper on the types so exactly, nor the man who bound it all up in this bright, red leather. And yet you know that such men were alive a short time ago; for the book was printed this year.

You very likely never will see these men, and yet you know they are alive somewhere.

Just so you know that God lives. For he made the cotton, which is here altered into paper; he made the oil and the wood, which are burned to make this ink; he made the skin of sheep, which is dressed, and colored, and is here in the shape of the morocco binding.

God knew you would love to see the light, and so he made the sun and the moon. He knew you would love to see beautiful things, and so he painted the rainbow in the dark clouds, and spread the green grass over the ground, and penciled the flowers, and planted the trees, and hung apples on one tree, and plums on another, and grapes on the vine. He knew you would love to hear sweet sounds, and so he gave your parents a pleasant voice, and filled the air with little birds, whose great business is to sing. He knew you would need houses and fires, and so he made the wood and the clay for the brick. He knew you would have reason, and yet not enough to lead you to heaven, and so he made the Bible. He knew you would have wicked hearts, and so he has given you the Sabbath, and the Savior, and the Holy Spirit, to help you to be good. He knew you would want to live forever, and so he has made heaven, where you may live forever, and never die, if you are good and holy, and trust in his Beloved Son.

Who does not see that the world is full of the things that God has done? I am sure I can no more doubt it than I can doubt that little boy to have eyes, when I see them both open and looking at me. I am sure I have no doubt that these children have souls, though I never saw their souls; for I can see their eyes, and hands and limbs moved by their souls.

And now, dear children, you see it all proved out to you that there is a great and glorious Being around you, always doing you good, whose name is God. Yes,

"There is an unseen Power around,
    Existing in the silent air:
Where treadeth man, where space is found,
    Unheard, unknown, that Power is there.

When sinks the pious Christian's soul,
    And scenes of horror daunt his eye,
He hears it whispered through the air,
    A Power of mercy still is nigh.

The Power that watches, guides, defends,
    Till man becomes a lifeless sod,
Till earth is nought,–nought earthly friends,–
    That omnipresent Power—is God."

Ought not these children to think of God? Ought you not to think of him when you go to bed at night, for he it is who has kept you safe and done you good all the day long, and then thank him for his goodness? Think of him in the morning, for it is he who has kept you, given you sleep and awaked you, and lifted up the great sun to shine upon you. Oh, pray that he will keep you from sinning all the day. You ought to think of him when you hear the pleasant and kind voice of your parents, for it is God who gave you these parents; think of him when you are happy, for it is he who makes you happy. Think of him when you have sinned, or are about to sin, for he sees you. Think of him when you are sick, for he only can make you well, and keep you from being sick. Think of him on the Sabbath, for he gave it to you to fit you for heaven. Yes, he gave you every good thing you ever had, or ever can have, and even gave his dear Son to die for sinners.

And now let me stop, after looking at each child before me, and repeating to each one this sincere wish of my heart –

"Oh, be thy wealth an upright heart;
    Thy strength, the sufferer's stay;
Thy earthly choice, the better part,
    Which cannot fade away:
Thy zeal for Christ, a quenchless fire;
    Thy friends, the men of peace;
Thy heritage, an angel's lyre,
    When earthly changes cease."

AMEN.

LECTURE III

REPENTANCE FOR SIN

"They went out and preached that men should repent."
- Mark 6.12

A hard word used. The hard word explained. Nothing good without pay. Who need repentance. Christ's testimony. Great question. Two kinds of money. Two trees. STORY. The sick father. Little boy's falsehood. The tender look. The dying father. Death arrived. The burial. Repentance at the grave. A few plain remarks. God not loved. The discontented boy—the storm—the Bible—his repentance. Who have sinned? Stopping in sin. The Indian and his rum. Hands full. Conclusion.

Children, I am going to use a hard word, and I must tell you what it means. The word is conditions. I would not use it if I did not think I could make it easy. Suppose a little child goes to school, and wants a new book. Her mother says, "Well, Mary, if you will be perfect in your lessons and behavior for two whole weeks, I will buy the book for you." This is a condition. A little boy asks his father to let him ride. He tells him he may ride with him tomorrow, on the condition, that he governs his temper and is a good boy all day today.

So every good thing in this world has some such condition, and for everything we have something to do. I will only name four things which have such conditions.

1. God has so ordered things that any child shall grow up greatly beloved and respected, on condition that he is kind and obedient to his parents and teachers, and kind and affectionate to every body.

2. God has so ordered things, that a man may be learned, on condition that he studies and reads, and wastes no time.

3.   God has so ordered things, that medicine will frequently cure the sick man. But the condition is that it must be carefully taken.

4.   God has so ordered things that anybody may know all about God, and heaven, on condition, that he faithfully reads the Bible, and prays to God for the Holy Spirit, and obeys God in everything.

It is just so with everything. Who would not laugh at the farmer who expected to raise corn, except on the condition that he plant, and hoe, and plant the right seed, and at the right time? That little boy cannot see his top spin round, except on a condition—that he do something to make it go. That little girl, just beginning to talk, cannot learn a single letter, or take a single stitch with her needle, except on condition that she try to learn. No. You cannot rear a single beautiful flower so as to get one single blossom, without a condition.

Now, the greatest good that God ever gave to us, is that eternal life which Christ bought for us by his own blood. No man ever became holy without a condition for him to fulfill. No man ever went to heaven without repentance. Job could not. David could not. Peter, and Paul, and John, could not. Not one of that great multitude who are now in heaven, went there without repentance. Christ preached this condition, and so did the apostles; so has every true preacher since. Not one sinner in this house, not one in this place, not one in this world, will ever go to heaven without repentance. If we knew just how many, and who would repent of sin, we should know just how many, and who would go to heaven. All must repent. Christ says, *"Except ye repent, ye shall all likewise perish."*[10] So Paul says, "God now commandeth all men everywhere to repent."[11] You cannot doubt who must repent—all must, every human being that has ever sinned.

---

[10] Luke 13:3,5.
[11] Acts 17:30.

A very great question rises up here; and that is, *"What is it to repent?"*

You all know there are two kinds of money—the good, and the counterfeit. And a man might have a house full of the counterfeit, and yet he could not be said to have any money. It would do him no good. So there are two kinds of repentance. One is good and the other good for nothing. They may not seem very different, just as two pieces of money may look alike, while one is good, and will buy things, and the other is good for nothing; just as two trees may stand together, and look alike, while one produces good fruit, and the other nothing but leaves. But you want to know what it is to repent. Let me try to tell you.

A man, who is now a minister of the gospel, gave me the following account. I tell it to you in order to show you what repentance is. "I had one of the kindest and best of fathers; and when I was a little white-headed boy, about six years old, he used to carry me to school before him on his horse, to help me in my little plans, and always seemed trying to make me happy; and he never seemed so happy himself as when making me happy. When I was six years old, he came home, one day, very sick. My mother, too, was sick; and thus nobody but my two sisters could take care of my father. In a few days he was worse, very sick, and all the physicians in the region were called in to see him. The next Sabbath morning, early, he was evidently much worse. As I went into the room, he stretched out his hand to me and said, 'My little boy, I am very sick. I wish you to take that paper on the stand, and run down to Mr. C.'s, and get me the medicine written on that paper.' I took the paper, and went to the apothecary's shop,[12] as I had often done before. It was about half a mile off; but when I got there, I found it closed; and as Mr. C. lived a quarter of

---

[12] The *apothecary* was the man who prepared and provided the medicine that was prescribed by the medical doctor.

28

a mile farther off, I concluded not to go to find him. I then set out for home. On my way back, I contrived what to say. I knew how wicked it was to tell a lie, but one sin always leads to another. On going in to my father, I saw that he was in great pain; and though pale and weak, I could see great drops of sweat standing on his forehead, forced out by the pain. Oh, then I was sorry I had not gone and found the apothecary. At length he said to me, 'My son has got the medicine, I hope, for I am in great pain.' I hung my head, and muttered, for my conscience smote me, 'No, sir, Mr. Carter says he has got none!'

'Has got none! Is this possible?' He then cast a keen eye upon me, and seeing my head hang, and probably suspecting my falsehood, said, in the mildest, kindest tone, *'My little boy will see his father suffer great pain for the want of that medicine!'* I went out of the room, and alone, and cried. I was soon called back. My brothers had come, and were standing,—all the children were standing, round his bed, and he was committing my poor mother to their care, and giving them his last advice. I was the youngest; and when he laid his hand on my head, and told me 'that in a few hours I should have no father; that he would in a day or two be buried; that I must now make God my father, love him, obey him, and always do right, and *speak the truth*, because the eye of God is always upon me'—it seemed as if I should sink; and when he laid his hand on my head again, and prayed for the blessing of God the Redeemer to rest upon me, 'soon to be a fatherless orphan,' I dared not look at him, I felt so guilty. Sobbing, I rushed from his bed-side, and thought I wished I could die. They soon told me he could not speak. Oh, how much would I have given to go in and tell him that I had told a lie, and ask him once more to lay his hand on my head and forgive me! I crept in once more, and heard the minister pray for 'the dying man.' Oh, how my heart ached! I snatched my hat, and ran to the apothecary's house, and got the medicine. I ran home with all my might, and ran in, and ran up to my father's bed-side to confess my sin, crying out, 'O here, father'—but I was hushed; and I then saw that he was pale, and that all in the room were weeping. *My dear father was dead!* And the last thing I ever spoke to him was *to tell him a lie!* I sobbed as if my heart would break; for his kindnesses, his tender looks, and my own sin, all rushed upon my mind. And as I gazed upon his cold, pale face, and saw his eyes shut, and his lips closed, could I help thinking of his last words, 'My little boy will see his father suffer great pain for the want of that medicine?' I could not know but he died for the lack of it.

"In a day or two, he was put into the ground and buried up. There were several ministers at the funeral, and each spoke kindly to me, but could not comfort me. Alas! they knew not what a load of sorrow lay on my heart. They could not comfort me. My father was buried, and the children all scattered abroad; for my mother was too feeble to take care of them.

"It was twelve years after this, while in college, that I went alone to the grave of my father. It took me a good while to find it; but there it was, with its humble tombstone; and as I stood over I seemed to be back at his bedside, to see his pale face, and hear his voice. Oh! the thought of that sin and wickedness cut me to the heart. It seemed as worlds would not be too much to give, could I then only have called loud enough to have him hear me ask his forgiveness. But it was too late. He had been in the grave twelve years; and I must live and die, weeping over that ungrateful falsehood. May God forgive me."

Now, I wish to say two or three things about this little boy's repentance.

1. You see that a child may be wicked. He can sin against a father and against God at the same time. God

commands us to obey our parents and to speak the truth. This child did neither.

2.   You see that a child is not too young to repent of a sin against his father. Some have an idea that a child is too young to repent; but this is a great mistake. If this boy could repent of this one sin, he could of more; and if he could repent of a sin against an earthly father, could he not of those against his heavenly Father?

3.   You see what true repentance towards God is. It is to feel sorry and grieved that you have sinned against God, just as this child did, because he had sinned against his dying father. He did not grieve so because he was afraid of being punished, but because his father was so good to him, and he was so wicked against his father. Now, had he felt as sorry for each and all of his sins against God, as he did for this *one* sin against a man, it would have been true repentance.

4.   You see that if we loved God as much as we do an earthly parent, we should repent deeply; because he has done us ten thousand kindnesses, and is doing them every day, and because we have committed ten thousand sins against him more shameful than this shameful sin of the little boy.

There was a wicked boy once, who would leave his father's home and go to sea. His kind father tried to persuade him not to go; but he was not to be kept away from the sea. The reason was, he thought that he might be wicked when he got away from his father, and there would be nobody to reprove him. His weeping father gave him a Bible as he went away, and begged him to read it. The boy went away, and became very wicked, and very profane. But God saw him. There was a great storm upon the ocean. The ship could not stand against it. She struck upon the rocks in the dark night. It was a time of great distress;—and for a few moments, there was the noise of the captain giving his orders, the howling of the storm, the cries of the poor sailors and passengers, who expected every moment to be drowned. Then this wicked boy wished himself at home. But he had but a few moments; for a great wave came and lifted the ship up high, and then came down upon another rock, and she was broken in a thousand pieces. Every soul on board was drowned, except this same wicked boy. By the mercy of God, he was washed and carried by the waves upon a great rock, so that he could creep up, much bruised and almost dead. In the morning, he was seen sitting on the rock with a book in his hand. It was his Bible,—the only thing, except his own life, which had been saved from the wreck. He opened it, and there, on the first page, was the hand-writing of his father! He thought of the goodness of that father, and of his own ingratitude, and he wept. Again he opened the book, and on every page was the handwriting of his heavenly Father; and again he wept at the remembrance of his sins against God. His heart was broken. He was truly penitent; and from that hour to this he has lived as a Christian. He is now the commander of a large ship, and seems to make it his great business to honor Jesus Christ. This was true repentance.

But I must tell you, in a few words, WHY it is necessary for every one to repent of sin.

1. *Because all have sinned.*[13] I need not try to tell how many times. I might as well try to count the hairs on that little boy's head, who stands at that pew door and gives me all his looks while I am speaking. We all have sinned against our parents, by not obeying them and being kind to them; we have sinned against the Sabbath, by not remembering to keep it holy; against the Bible, by not loving it and not keeping its sayings; against conscience, which stands close to our heart, and, like a sentinel keeping watch, cries out when we sin; against the Holy Spirit, by not doing as he says, when he makes us feel solemn and sinful; and against God himself, whose commandments we break. Oh! our sins are like a great cloud. Did you ever see a cloud of dust or sand in a windy day? And could you count the little particles of dust in it—all of them? No, no. But our sins are quite as many.

2. *None will forsake sin till they have repented.* You might stop a man from stealing by killing him or shutting him up in prison. But this would not stop his wishing to steal; and that wishing, in the sight of God, is sin. One of these children might have his tongue cut out, so that he could not talk, and so that he could never again tell a lie; but if he thought a lie in his heart, this would be sin; and cutting out his tongue would not stop his sinning. The Indians, some years ago, tried to stop their people from sinning; and so they gave them strong emetics,[14] in order to have them throw up their sins; but they did no good. The sin was in the heart, and not in the stomach. One of these Indians, who had thus taken emetics, went to Pittsburgh, and bought a barrel of rum to sell to the other Indians. On

---

[13] Romans 3:23.

[14] Emetics produce nausea and vomiting, and their use is limited to the treatment of poisoning with certain toxins that have been swallowed.

his way back, he called and heard the Moravian[15] missionaries preach the gospel. "He was so convinced of his sinfulness and misery that he resolved to alter his manner of life. He accordingly returned the barrel of rum to the trader at Pittsburgh, declaring that he would neither drink nor sell any more spirituous liquors, for it was against his conscience. He, therefore, begged him to take it back, adding, that, if he refused, he would pour it into the Ohio River. The trader, as well as the white people who were present, were amazed, and assured him, that this was the first barrel of rum he had ever seen returned by an Indian: but he, at the same time, took it back, without further objection."

Nothing but repentance would ever have led this Indian to do this. And this, and nothing but this, will make any one leave off sin.

3. *None will serve God unless they have first repented of sin.* Christ says that no man can serve two masters. Suppose a child has a large apple in each hand, and, without laying down either, she goes and tries to take up two large oranges. Could she do it? No. Because her hands are already full. Just so, when the heart is full of sin, you cannot have the love of God in it. If you would stop sinning, my dear children, you must repent of sin. If you would serve God, have him for your Father and Friend, you must repent. You all can do it. You all have been sorry when you have grieved your parents, and you can be sorry when you have offended and grieved your blessed Redeemer. Oh! if you will not, you will grow up sinners, live sinners, die sinners, and be sinners, accursed by God for ever and ever. May it never be so with any of you who read these words. Amen.

---

[15] Moravians or Bohemian Brethren was a religious community tracing its origin from John Huss, expelled by persecution from Bohemia and Moravia in the eighteenth century. They are often called The United Brethren.

LECTURE IV

ANGELS' JOY WHEN SINNERS REPENT

There is joy in the presence of the angels of God
over one sinner that repenteth. –Luke 15:10.

Who ever saw an angel? What angels do. Many angels. How do they feel? Why they rejoice. First reason. Home. Whom have they seen? The poor boy. What is an eye worth? What is the soul worth? The second reason. The sick child. The little boy drowning. The boy recovered. The brazen serpent. Three remarks. What people talk about. Piece of gold. What men love. Sleeping out of doors. Bitter medicine. The broken arm. The last remark.

Did any of these children ever see an angel? No. Did I ever see one? No. Did anybody ever see an angel? Yes. A great many have. Abraham did. Lot did. David did. Christ did. Peter and John did. And in the Bible you read of many who have seen angels.

But though you never *saw* an angel, yet you all know what an angel is. Angels are good spirits, who love God more than they love one another, and more than they love anything else. They live in heaven. And what do you think they are doing there? Idle, do you think? No. They are never idle a moment. Sometimes God sends them away on errands, just as your parents send you. Sometimes they come down to this world to do good to good people here. When a good man dies, they stand by his bed, and carry his soul up to heaven, just as you are led by the hand when you do not know the way.

And though we cannot see them, yet I suppose some are here in this meeting-house now, seeing you and me, and looking to see if this sermon will do any good. What else do

35

they do? Why, if God has no errands on which to send them, then they sing his praises, and make music a thousand times sweeter than any which we ever heard.

There are a great many of these angels in heaven;—more than this house would hold,—more than a thousand or a million of such meeting-houses would hold, if they were all to be seated just as you are. And, they are all happy. Because not one of them ever did wrong; not one ever spoke a cross or a wicked word; not one of them ever told a lie; not one of them ever sinned, or ever felt any kind of pain. And, what is very wonderful, they love us. They come down here, and when anybody repents of sin, they tell of it in heaven, and they all rejoice and are glad. Now, just read this beautiful text again. "I say unto you, there is joy in the presence of the angels of God over one sinner that repenteth." Now, if I had told you this without first finding it in God's Book, you could not have believed me. But now we know it *must* be so, because Christ hath told us so; and he says, "Heaven and earth shall pass away, but my words shall not pass away."[16]

I wish, now, my dear children, to tell you two plain reasons why the angels rejoice over every sinner who repents. I could give you many more reasons, but am afraid you cannot remember more.

First, then, they rejoice when any one repents, because *they know what heaven and hell are.*

Now, suppose I had never seen any one of you before; and I should ask one of these little boys or girls about their home. You could tell me about it—where you eat, where you sleep, where you play, how you are kept warm in the cold weather,—how your parents take good care of you,—where you go to school,—how many ways your parents take to make you happy. You could tell me all about your home, and your garden, and all your pleasant things there, *because you have always lived there.*

---

[16] Matthew 24:35; Mark 13:31; Luke 21:33.

Just so of the angels. They have always lived in heaven, and know how pleasant a place it is. And when any one repents, they know he will go to heaven, and be happy as they are. They have talked with good old Noah about the wicked world that was drowned in the flood, when he,

"humble, happy saint,
Surrounded with the chosen few,
Sat in the ark, secure from fear,
And sang the grace that steered him through!"

They have talked with Abraham, and Joseph, and David, and Paul, and all the happy men in heaven; and they know that they are all happy, and so they rejoice when any one repents and sets out to go to heaven.

Suppose you were to see a poor ragged boy, almost frozen with the cold, and who has no home, and no fire to warm him by, and no food to eat, and no bed to sleep on, and no friends to take care of him; now, would you not be glad to have some kind man take that poor child in, and give him a good home like yours? Yes. I know you would—I know you would, because you know what it is to have a pleasant home. Well, just so the blessed angels feel when any one repents, for they know God will take him to heaven.

Children, what would you let any one take some heavy tool and crush your finger for? For a dollar? No. For ten? No. But what would you have your arm cut off for? For a hundred dollars? No. For all the playthings in the whole world? No. For how much would you lose your *reason,* and be crazy? For anything in this world? No. I know you would not. For how much would you have your eyes put out, so that you could never again see your friends, nor the beautiful light of the glorious sun? Not for all the world. But, my dear children, the man who goes to hell because he will not repent of sin, is worse off

37

than if he were to lose an arm, or his eyes; yes, worse off than if he were to lose his reason, or be put into the fire, and. kept burning all day, and all night, and a year, and ten thousand years. For he loses his soul, and has not a friend in heaven, nor anywhere else; and, what is more, he never will have a friend. He is "covered with shame and everlasting contempt."[17] The holy angels know all this, and rejoice when any sinner repents, and thus escapes the punishment of hell. This is the first reason. Can you remember it?

2. The second reason why angels rejoice over a sinner who repents, is, that *till he does repent, it is very uncertain whether he ever will.*

If one of you were sick, and laid on the bed, and were so sick that it was very uncertain whether you would live or die, your parents and friends would feel very anxious about you. They would come to your bed-side, and raise up your feeble head, and inquire about your pain, and send off for the physician, and would sit up with you all night. Yes, and they would think more about their sick child, and feel more anxious about you, than about all the rest of the family, so long as it was uncertain whether or not you got well. And just so the angels feel, so long as it is uncertain whether or not a sinner repents.

Turn now to the 12th chapter of 2 Samuel, and see if David did not feel just so. As long as it was uncertain whether his child should live or die, he lay on the ground, and fasted and prayed. This uncertainty made him feel very anxious.

Suppose one of your little brothers should fall into the river, and there sink down under the deep waters, and before he could be gotten out, he should grow cold, and pale, and seem to be dead. Your father takes the little boy in his arms, and carries him home, and then they wrap

---

[17] Daniel 12:2.

38

him up in warm flannels, and lay him on the bed. The doctor comes, and goes into the room with your father and mother, to see if it is possible to save the little boy's life. The doctor says that nobody may go into the room but the parents. They go in, and shut the door, and in *a few* minutes the question is to be decided, whether or not the child can live. Oh, then, how would you go to the door, and walk around with a step soft as velvet, and hearken to know whether the dear boy lives! And after you had listened for some time, treading softly, and speaking in whispers, and breathing short, the door opens, and your mother comes out, and there are tears in her eyes! Is he dead?—says one, in a faint, sinking whisper —is he dead? Oh, no—no—your little brother lives, and will be well again! Oh, what a thrill of joy do you all feel! What leaping up in gladness! Now, there is such a joy in heaven over one sinner that repenteth. The sinner has been sick, but the gospel has been taken as the remedy, and he is to live forever. Do you wonder that the angels rejoice at it?

Just turn to the 21st chapter of Numbers, and read the account of the healing of those who had been bitten by the fiery serpents. Had you been there, you might have seen parents carrying their little children who had been bitten, and who were just ready to die. The poison of the serpents is circulating through them, and they are almost gone. The mother brings up her child to the brazen serpent. Oh, how anxious is she, lest it has not got strength sufficient to look up! How tenderly does she gaze upon its face, as she holds it up to the brazen serpent, waiting for it to open its eyes! and what joy when it does look up and live! So there is joy in the presence of the angels of God over one sinner that repenteth.

I have now told you the two reasons why the holy angels rejoice when a sinner repents. I next wish you to hear *three* remarks. Will you remember them—all three?

1. Most men are not like the holy angels.

By being *like* the angels, I do not mean, that most men do not *look* like them; for nobody looks like them. But I mean that they do not *feel* like them. You hear men talk every day. What do they talk about? Why, about the weather, their health, their cattle, their crops, their farms, and their neighbors; but very few say anything about the repentance of sinners.

Suppose one of you should repent today. I should be glad, and so would some others; but the greater part of the people in this town would know nothing about it; or, if they did, they would care nothing about it. Not so with the angels. They would all rejoice over it—would all know it. Suppose one of you should find a piece of gold, as you go home, as big as your fist. What a wonder! All the town would know of it, and talk about it, and call you a lucky child; but the angels would care nothing about it—no, not if you should find gold enough to fill this house. You see why. Because they feel for your soul; while most men think only of this world. And the reason is, men are sinners, and most of them love anything better than repentance. If any one of you should repent today, I suppose many would laugh and sneer at it. But not an angel in heaven would laugh or sneer. You see, then, how it is, that the first remark is true, that most men are not like the holy angels.

2. My second remark is *that we cannot go to heaven without repenting of sin.*

If a man could go to heaven without repenting of sin, then nobody would need to repent; and if any one did repent, he would be doing what was not needful. And if so, then the angels would rejoice to see men do what they need not do!

Suppose I should say to you today, that, in order to meet God on the Sabbath, and receive God's blessing, you must sleep out on the ground all Saturday night, wet or cold, sick or well. Suppose you do it, and I rejoice to see you do it. Now, if this be *not* necessary in order to receive God's blessing, then it would be cruel in me to wish to see you doing it.

You know, when you are sick, your parents rejoice to see you swallow, cheerfully, the bitter medicine, because you cannot get well without taking it; but if you could get well just as well without, your parents would never rejoice to see you take it. Now, repentance is disliked as much as medicine is; and if we could go to heaven without it, the holy angels would not rejoice to see us repenting.

Suppose, in going home today, one of you should break his arm so dreadfully that it must be cut off, or else you die; and I should call and see you tomorrow, and should find the doctor there, with his sharp tools all out, ready to cut the arm off, I should rejoice to have it cut off! And why?

Not, my dear children, because I should love to see you suffer, or lose your arm; but because your life could not be saved without. And thus you see why the angels rejoice so much over one who repents. It is because none can go to heaven without repentance.

3. My third and last remark is, *that you will all be very wicked if you do not repent immediately.*

And why? Because you are all sinners; and because I have read to you Christ's words, how that the angels would rejoice at it, and have told you *why* they would rejoice. No one is too young to sin, and so it is plain that no one is too young to repent. Because, too, that if you do not repent, you cannot go to heaven. You can play, you may grow up, you may learn your books, you may become rich, if God spares your lives; and may do all this without repentance. But, you cannot go to heaven without it. You cannot begin to go, till you have a new heart.

And now, when you are riding or walking home, not knowing that you will live to see another Sabbath; when you see the sun go down today, not knowing as you will live to see him rise; as you lie down to sleep tonight, not knowing that you will ever open your eyes again in this world,—will you not remember what I have now told you, and go before God and repent! Oh, if you will, there will be joy in heaven over you. Amen.

LECTURE V

WHAT FAITH IS, AND WHAT ITS USE IS

Without faith it is impossible to please him—Heb. 11.6.

Lecture to be made plain. Different kinds of faith. The little girl who was generous. Faith rewarded, and made plain. The glass beads. Faith in a father. The storm at sea. Faith in God. Casting bread on the waters. Sowing rice. The old man and his son. The house of the slave. The mother's faith. Faith in Christ. Falling into the river. Faith leads to obey God—to do good. The dying mother. Faith comforts us. The dead boy's lantern.

I am going to make this Lecture very plain, and, I hope, very interesting to these children. You may, at first, suppose it will be about what you cannot understand, and that it cannot be interesting to you. But let us see. I do not believe there will be five of these children who will not hear it all, and remember most of what I shall now say.

There are many kinds of faith or belief among men. But only one kind is the true faith, without which it is impossible to please God, because only one kind of faith makes us obey God. I will explain it to you.

A little girl was once walking with her father, and they were talking together. They were talking about being *generous*. The father told the little girl that it meant "to give to others what would do them good, even if we had to go without ourselves." He also told her, that generous people were happy; because nobody could deny himself anything, in order to give it to another, without feeling happy;—so that no one ever lost anything by being generous, because God would make him happy for doing

43

so. He then asked her if she *believed* this. She said, "Yes, father." In the course of their walk, they went into a bookstore. The little girl said, "Father, I want one of these new books very much." "So do I," said the father; "but I cannot afford to buy each of us one. But here is some money; and you may do just as you please; you may buy a book, and give to your father, and go without yourself, or you may buy one for yourself, and I will go without. Do just as you please." The little girl hung her head, and looked at the new books; but then she thought of what her father had said about being *generous,* and she had *faith* in his words. She quickly said, "I will go without, and father shall have the book." The book was therefore bought. And the child felt happy, because she had believed her father, and because she had been generous. The bookseller, however, overheard the conversation, and was so much pleased at seeing the *faith* and the generosity of the little girl, that he gave her a very beautiful book.

This was having faith in a father. But this is not the kind of faith spoken of in the Bible. For a child might believe a father, and have a strong faith in him, and yet be, towards God, a very wicked child.

Mr. Cecil gives us a beautiful account of the manner in which he taught his little daughter what is meant by faith. "She was playing one day with a few beads, which seemed to delight her wonderfully. Her whole soul was absorbed in her beads. I said,

'My dear, you have some pretty beads there.'

'Yes, papa.'

'And you seem to be vastly pleased with them.'

'Yes, papa.'

'Well, now, throw them into the fire.'

The tears started into her eyes. She looked earnestly at me, as though she ought to have a reason for such a cruel sacrifice.

'Well, my dear, do as you please; but you know I never told you to do anything which I did not think would be good for you.'

She looked at me a few moments longer, and then—summoning up all her fortitude her breast heaving with the effort—she dashed them into the fire.

'Well,' said I; 'there let them lie; you shall hear more about them another time; but say no more about them now.'

Some days after, I bought her a box full of larger beads, and toys of the same kind. When I returned home, I opened the treasure, and set it before her; she burst into tears of ecstasy. 'Those, my child,' said I, 'are yours; because you believed me, when I told you it would be better for you to throw those two or three paltry beads into the fire. Now, that has brought you this treasure. But now, my dear, remember, as long as you live, what FAITH is. You threw your beads away when I bid you, because you had faith in me, that I never advised you but for your good. Put the same confidence in God. Believe everything he says in his Word. Whether you understand it or not, have faith in him that he means your good.'"

This, too, was faith in a father; but the little girl might have had it, even if she had been a heathen child. It was not the faith required in the Bible, because it was not faith in God himself.

I will now tell you what is faith in the *care* of God. A lady and her husband were standing on the deck of a ship during an awful storm. The winds howled, and the ship was tossed like a feather over the great waves. The lady had to hold on with both hands to keep from falling. She was very much frightened, and asked her husband if he was not afraid. He said nothing, but, in a moment after, he held a naked sword with its point close to her breast, and asked her,

"Are you not afraid?"

"No."

45

"Why not? Do you see this sword within an inch of your heart?"

"Yes, but I am not afraid, for it is my husband who holds it!"

"Yes," said he, "and it is my heavenly Father who holds this storm in his hand, the winds and the waves; and why should I be afraid? No, I am not afraid!"

This was faith in the care of God. God was pleased with it. Now see. Was not the gentleman pleased to see that his wife had so much faith in his love as not to be afraid, though he held a drawn sword to her heart? Yes, he must have been pleased. And so was God pleased to see him put so much faith in his care, when the storm was raging, and the ship seemed like being destroyed.

The Bible tells us to "cast our bread upon the waters, and we shall find it after many days."[18] Let us see what this text means. Rice is the food most used in the Eastern countries, especially in Egypt, even to this day. Every year, when the snows all melt off the mountains, the river Nile rises up high, and overflows its banks, and covers all the country round it with waters. The people set down stakes, every man in his own land, before the waters come. And when the Nile has risen, and all the ground is covered with waters, they go out in their little boats, and sow, or cast their rice upon the waters. The rice sinks down, and sticks in the mud beneath; and when the waters are gone, they find it has taken root and sprouted, and it grows up, and gives them a harvest. This is casting their bread upon the waters, and finding it after many days.

Here is one kind of faith. The man who sows the rice, believes that it will sink, that the waters will go off in due time, and that he shall come out and find his rice growing. This is a kind of faith in the Providence of God.

---

[18] Ecclesiastes 11:1.

But, you know, this is not the faith required in the Bible, because a very wicked man has faith to plant and sow, expecting to get a harvest, though he forgets that God must make every blade to grow, if it does grow. Thousands have had this kind of faith, but it did not make them good and holy.

Now, let me show you what *faith in God* is,—such a faith as will please God.

There was once a man to whom God spoke, and told him to leave his home, his town, and his country, and go off into a strange land, and live under a tent, and never again have a home. The man asked no reasons, but obeyed. After this, he had a son, his only son. God told him that this son should live and grow up, and should be the forefather of great nations, millions of people. But after this, God told this man to go and take this boy of his, and take his life, and burn up his body with fire. God gave him no reasons for this direction. The good man prepared to obey. He got the wood ready to burn the body of his dear child; he bound his hands and feet, and put out his hand, and took the knife with which to take his life. God then told him not to do it, but to take a ram which he would find close by, and kill him. This was faith in God; for Abraham (for that was his name, and you will find the whole account in the 22nd chapter of Genesis) obeyed God, because he believed God was wise, and holy, and good, though he could not understand why he told him to do this.

Suppose you had lived while the children of Israel lived in Egypt. And suppose you had walked out some pleasant day, just at night, down towards the river. Look, now, and see what is before you. Yonder is a cluster of tall trees, and just under them is a little cottage or hovel. They are poor folks who live there. See, the house is small, and has no paint on it, no windows, nothing about it that looks

47

comfortable. This hovel is the home of slaves. The man and the woman are poor slaves. But just look inside. What is that woman doing? See her weaving a little basket with rushes, which she has gathered from the banks of the river. See! She weeps as she twists every flag; and, by the moving of her lips, you see that she is praying. She has finished it. Now, watch her. Do you see her go to the corner of the room, and there kneel down, and weep, and pray over a beautiful little boy? See her embrace and kiss him. Now she lays him in the little basket; now she calls her little daughter, and tells her to take her little brother, and carry him, and lay him down by the cold river's side! There! now she takes the last look of her sweet babe; now she goes back weeping into the house, and lifting her heart to God in prayer, while her daughter goes, and carries her dear boy, and leaves him on the bank of the river. What will become of him? Will the crocodiles eat him up? or will the waters carry him off and drown him? No, no. That poor mother has FAITH in God; and God will take care of her son. The king's daughter will find him, and save him; and that little infant is to be Moses, the leader of Israel, the prophet of God, and the writer of much of the Bible! This was true faith in God.

Faith in Jesus Christ is a strong belief in him; such a belief as will lead us to obey his commands. We believe there was such a being on earth once as Christ; that he did the miracles told of in the Testament; that he was holy; that he spoke the words and the sermons told of in the Testament, as coming from him; that he died for sinners, and rose from the dead, and is gone to heaven, and now lives there, and is doing good to his people. We believe all that is told us about him in the Bible. And if this belief or faith is good for anything, it will cause us to love to read the Bible, to obey Christ, to love him and to serve him, because he will reward his people forever beyond the grave, and punish those who do not obey him.

Suppose, as a good old writer says, you should fall into a river, which was deep, and where the water ran swiftly, and you were almost drowned; and a man should run to the bank of the river, and call to you, and throw you a rope. This would be just like our Savior. We are all perishing in the "deep waters" of sin; and Christ throws us the rope, and calls to us to take hold of it. But it will all do no good unless we take hold of it. Now, this taking hold of the rope *is faith*. Faith makes us take hold of Christ, just as you would take hold of the rope, when drowning. He draws us from the deep waters; and when he has done it, we love him, we thank him, and we obey him.

But I wish to tell you, in a few words, what good faith does us.

1. *It makes us obey and serve God.* No one will serve God by leaving off sin and doing his will, unless he has faith to believe that he will reward all who are good, and punish all who remain wicked. Who would get any good from the Bible, if they have not faith in it? Who would try to govern the temper, the tongue, the words, and the thoughts, if they did not believe that God will bring every secret thing unto judgment?[19] No one. But if we believe what God has told us in his Word, we shall be very careful to do what God commands us to do. The sailor goes away on the great waters, and works hard and faithfully, because he has faith to believe the captain will pay him. So we must have faith in the promises of God, if we would serve him and please him.

2. *Faith makes us do good.* The apostles went everywhere preaching the gospel, though they were hated, and stoned, and put in prison, and put to death, because they believed God, and had faith in his Word, that whoever will repent,

---

[19] Ecclesiastes 12:14; Romans 2:16.

and love Christ, shall be saved; and whoever will not, shall be lost forever. It is the faith which led them to endure such sufferings, that lead good men now to go to the heathen, and preach to them, and die among them. It is faith in God that leads good men to preach, to have Bible Societies, and to make great efforts, and take great pains, to have all men everywhere know, and believe, and obey the Bible. It is this faith which leads the praying mother to come to the bed of her little child, and hear him say his prayers before he shuts his eyes in sleep. It is faith that comforts the dying mother as she leaves this world, and leaves her dear children behind without any mother. I once visited a dying mother, who had this faith in Christ; and after she had called her children around her bed, and had taken each one by the hand, and had given each her advice and her blessing, and had bidden them farewell, and was then too much exhausted to speak aloud,

> "She made a sign
> to bring her babe; 'twas brought, and by her placed.
> She looked upon its face, that neither smiled
> Nor wept, nor knew who gazed upon it; and laid
> Her hand upon its little breast, and sought
> For it—with look that seemed to penetrate
> The heavens—unutterable blessings—such
> As God to dying parents only granted
> For infants left behind them in the world.
> 'God bless my child!' we heard her say, and heard
> No more. The angel of the covenant
> Was come; and, faithful to his promise, stood,
> Prepared to walk with her through death's dark vale.
> And now her eyes grew bright, and brighter still,—
> Too bright for ours to look upon, suffused
> With many tears,—and closed without a cloud.
> They set as sets the morning star, which goes
> Not down behind the darkened west, nor hides
> Obscured among the tempests of the sky,—
> But melts away into the light of heaven!"

3. *Faith comforts us, and holds us up, in the time of trouble.*
There are many times when we can have no help from any
human friend. None but God can aid us. It was so with
Noah, when the ark floated upon the great waters, and
nobody but God could roll off these waters, and make the
dry land appear. It was so with Daniel, when thrown among
the fierce lions, and nobody could shut their mouths but
God. It is so with every dying Christian, whether he dies at
home among his friends, or away from home among
strangers, or alone where no one is with him. See what faith
can do for a child, and in the most awful situation:

"By a sudden burst of water into one of the Newcastle
collieries,[20] thirty-five men and forty-one lads were driven
into a distant part of the pit, from which there was no
possibility of return, until the water should be drawn off.
While this was effecting, though all possible means were
used, the whole number died, from starvation or
suffocation. When the bodies were drawn up from the pit,
seven of the youth were discovered in a cavern separate
from the rest. Among these was one, of peculiarly moral
and religious habits, whose daily reading the Sacred
Scriptures to his widowed mother, when he came up from
his labors, had formed the solace of her lonely condition.
After his funeral, a sympathizing friend of the neglected
poor went to visit her; and while the mother showed him,
as a relic of her son, his Bible, worn and soiled with
constant perusal, he happened to cast his eyes on a candle-
box, with which, as a miner, he had been furnished, and
which had been brought up from the pit with him; and
there he discovered the following affecting record of the
filial affection and steadfast piety of the youth. In the darkness of the suffocating pit, with a bit of pointed iron, he

---

[20] Coal mining is the mining of coal. Colliery refers to the mine, and the
associated buildings and machinery.

had engraved on the box his last message to his mother, in these words:

'Fret not, my Dear Mother, for we were singing and praising God while we had time. Mother, follow God more than I did. Joseph, be a good lad to God and mother.'"

This was faith; and, oh, what comfort did it give this poor boy in the hour of dying! And what comfort to the poor widow, as she wept over her dear son! May you, dear children, all have such a faith. Amen.

LECTURE VI

GOD WILL TAKE CARE OF US

Consider the lilies of the field, how they grow; they toil not,
neither do they spin. And yet I say unto you, that even Solomon,
in all his glory, was not arrayed like one of these.
–Matt.6.28,29.

How Christ preached. The rich man. God is very rich. Hogshead of gold.
Many cattle. Servants. Little boy and his sister. Charge to angels, and
beautiful illustration. The garden lily. The cold winter and the lily. The pond.
Sermon by a lily. The poor heathen child. His lonely feelings. Comes to
America. His death. Sailing of the missionaries. The hymn. The gospel
received. The weeping mother. The ostrich in the wilderness. Sorrows to
come. When will God be a friend?

Our Savior used to preach anywhere, and everywhere, as
he met with those who wanted to hear him. Sometimes he
sat down on the ground, and sometimes sat in the boat on
the water, and sometimes stood in the great temple and
preached. He used to be very plain, and easy to be understood. He would have preached finely to children; and if he
were now to speak to all these children before me, I do not
believe there is a single one who would not understand all
he should say. And yet it is possible, if any one wants to do
so, to misunderstand even the Savior himself. Now see.
Suppose a lazy boy should read over my text, and then say,
that Christ teaches us that God takes care of the lilies,
though they do no work, and, therefore, we need not work,
and he will take care of us in our idleness. This would be to
make the Bible favor our sins; but the Bible never does that.

53

Suppose you should go and visit a man who was so rich that he had his trees covered with silk of the most beautiful colors, and even his most ugly looking creatures covered with gold and silver, and adorned by the most curious art! Would you not think him a rich man? And if he were known to be a good man, and true to his word, and he should tell you that he would be your friend, and always take care of you, would you have any fear but he would do it?

God is richer than all this. He is so rich that he can put more of what is beautiful upon a single lily or tulip, than the great king Solomon could put on all his clothing. The hoarse, homely peacock carries more that is beautiful upon his tail than the richest king could ever show. And even the poor butterfly, which is to live but a few hours, has a more glorious dress than the proudest, richest man that ever lived. God can afford to dress this poor worm up so, because he is rich. If, then, he can afford to take such care of the lilies, the birds, and insects, and to make them more beautiful than man can ever be, will he not take care of us, if we obey him?

Suppose you had a rich father—so rich that he had a hogshead[21] full of gold, and a great barn full of silver. Do you think that, if you were to be a good child, he would ever refuse to take care of you? But God has more gold and silver laid up in the ground, which men have not yet dug up, than would make a mountain—it may be a hundred mountains. Can he not take care of you?

Suppose your father had more oxen, and horses, and cattle, than you could count over in a day, or in a week. Would he not be able to take care of his child, and give him everything he needs? Yes. But God has "cattle upon ten thousand hills," and "every beast of the forest" is his, and his

---

[21] *Hogshead* is a British unit of capacity for alcoholic beverages, at least 63 gallons, and thus speaks of a very large amount of gold.

"are all the fowls of the air!"[22] Can he not give you food from all these cattle, and clothe you, and give you beds from the feathers of all these fowls? Yes, he is able to do it all.

Suppose your father was so rich that he had ten thousand men at work for him every day, all at work, and all paid to their satisfaction, and all happy in working for him. Would you have any fears but he could take care of you, and do you good? But God has more servants than these. He has all the good people on earth in his employment, and all the angels in heaven. He pays them all. And if you need anything, he can send one, or a million of these his servants to you, to help you.

A little boy asked his mother to let him lead his little sister out on the green grass. She had just begun to run alone, and could not step over anything that lay in the way. His mother told him he might lead out the little girl, but *charged* him not to let her fall. I found them at play, very happy, in the field.

---

[22] Psalm 50:10,11.

I said, "You seem very happy, George. Is this your sister?"

"Yes, sir."

"Can she walk alone?"

"Yes, sir, on smooth ground."

"And how did she get over these stones, which lie between us and the house?"

"O, sir, mother *charged* me to be careful that she did not fall, and so I put my hands under her arms, and lifted her up when she came to a stone, so that she need not hit her little foot against it."

"That is right, George. And I want to tell you one thing. You see now how to understand that beautiful text, 'He shall give his angels charge concerning thee, lest at any time thou dash thy foot against a stone.'[23] God charges his angels to lead and lift good people over difficulties, just as you have lifted little Anne over these stones. Do you understand it now?"

"O yes, sir, and I shall never forget it while I live."

Can one child thus take care of another, and cannot God take care of those who put their trust in him? Surely he can; and there is not a child among you here today, over whom he is not ready to give his holy angels charge.

Did you never see the lily as it stands in the garden in the summer? God sends it the pure sunshine, and it seems to rejoice in his warm beams. He sends it the cooling dews, and it seems to drink in their sweetness like milk. The clouds gather, the storm rages, the rains pour down, the winds sweep along. See! the lily has shut up its blossom, and folded its leaves, and meekly bows its head, and bends to the wind, and asks no eye to gaze on it, while the storm lasts. God has taught it to do thus, till the smile shall again follow the tempest. It is not injured. It opens and smiles again. So does God teach the good. The Christian thus

---

[23] Psalm 91:11,12; cf. Matthew 4:6; Luke 4:10,11.

rejoices when blessed; and when troubles and sorrows come, he meekly bows and waits till God remembers him and removes the storm.

You have seen the lily, in the fall, when the frosts came, drop its head, and droop, and die. The stalk on which the sweet flower waved all summer, is gone, and the spot where it stood is forgotten. But see the care of God for that lily. The cold winter goes past, the sunshine of spring returns, the young buds swell and open, and the lily, which has only been sleeping in the ground, puts up its meek head, and rises again to beauty and glory. God takes care of the frail, beautiful plant, and will not let it perish forever. So you have seen the beautiful little child, which stood, like the flower in the garden, struck down by sickness, and cut down by death, and laid in the little grave. But God will take care of it. The long winter will be over; and though that dear child is forgotten by every body on earth, yet it is not forgotten by God. There is a day coming when God will come down from heaven, and send his angel to call this child from the long sleep of the grave, and it will come up from the ground fair and glorious on the morning of the great day.[24] Do you ask how it can be? Let me ask you one question.

Did you ever see a pond covered over with hard ice, thick and cold, all the long winter? Well, the spring comes, and the ice melts away, and the lily-seed, which has so long been sleeping in the mud at the bottom of the pond, springs up, and shoots up, and opens its beautiful white flower, on the top of the smooth water, and seems to smile as it looks up towards heaven. How is this done? By the care and the power of that God who watches over all his

---

[24] Dr. Todd does not mean that the soul of the child sleeps until the Day of Judgment, but rather that his body sleeps in the grave until that Day. As the Lord Jesus told the dying thief, "This day you shall be with me in Paradise." See Luke 23:43; cf. 2 Corinthians 5:8; Philippians 1:21-23.

works, and who will take care of the flower-seed, and of the immortal spirit of every child.

While too many people, who know about God, seem to live, day after day, for years, without loving, or obeying, or even speaking of God, you can almost hear the lily speak, as if preaching, and say,—

"I acknowledge the presence of God, my Maker. When he passes by me on the soft wings of the breeze, I wave my head as he passes; when he rides on the whirlwind or the storm, I bow and tremble; when he draws over me the curtains of the night, I feel safe, and go to sleep; when he opens upon me the eye of morning, I wake up, and drink in the fresh beams of his sun; and when he sends his chilling frosts, I let my frail body perish, and hide myself in the ground, knowing that he will again raise me up to life and beauty!"

Some years ago, there was a poor child left alone, at the death of his parents, in a distant island of the ocean. His people were all heathen, wicked people. His father and mother were killed in a cruel war. Now, see how God takes care of his creatures. Let us hear his own account of the thing. "At the death of my parents, I was with them; I saw them killed with a bayonet—and with them my little brother, not more than two or three months old—so that I was left alone without father or mother in this wilderness world. Poor boy, thought I within myself, after they were gone, are there any father or mother of mine at home, that I may go and find them at home? No; poor boy am I. And while I was at play with other children, after we had made an end of playing, they return to their parents,—but I was returned into tears,—for I have no home, neither father nor mother. I was now brought away from my home to a stranger place, and I thought of nothing more but my lack of father or mother, and I cried day and night. While I was with my uncle, for some time I began to think about leaving that country, to go to some other part of the globe. I thought to myself that if I should get away, and go to some other country; probably I may find some comfort, more than to live there, without father and mother."

This poor boy, thus left, an orphan, in a heathen country, was under the care of God. He left the island, and came to this country. Here he found kind friends, who took care of him, and taught him to read and write, and who took great pains to teach him about God and about Jesus Christ. He became a true Christian, and a dear youth he was. He wanted to go back to his country, to tell his people about God and Jesus; but just as he had gotten his education, and was ready, he was taken sick, and died. His name was HENRY OBOOKIAH.[25] He died with "a hope full of immortality." His grave is in Cornwall, Connecticut. But he lived not in vain. By means of his life and death, good men felt so much for his poor countrymen, that many good missionaries have gone to those islands, and there built churches, and printed school books, opened schools, printed the Bible, and taught many thousands to read and to know God. The foolish idols are destroyed, and they are becoming a Christian nation.

I remember when the missionaries first set out for that country. They sailed from New Haven; and before they entered the ship, and as they took leave of their dear friends, amid a great company of Christians, they all united in singing a beautiful hymn.[26] Three verses of this I will now read to you.

> "Wake, isles of the South! your redemption is near;
> No longer repose in the borders of gloom;
> The strength of his chosen in love will appear,
> And light shall arise on the verge of the tomb.

---

[25] Henry Obookiah (1792-1818) was born in Hawaii. His memoir was written in 1818 by the American Tract Society, written by Rev. E.W. Dwight.
[26] This hymn was written by William B. Tappan (1794-1849), a man who wrote many hymns including *'Tis Midnight and on Olive's Brow.*

The heathen will hasten to welcome the time,
The day-spring, the prophet in vision once saw,
When the beams of Messiah will 'lumine each clime,
And the isles of the ocean shall wait for his law

And thou, OBOOKIAH, now sainted above,
Shalt rejoice as the heralds their mission disclose;
And thy prayers shall be heard, that the land thou didst love
May blossom as Sharon, and bud as the rose!"

Oh! what care and goodness in God, thus to guide this lonely child to this country, and, by his means, lead many to go and carry the gospel to that whole nation! The Sabbath is now known there, and many thousands have already learned to read the Word of God; and we believe multitudes have become true Christians, and have followed Henry to the presence of God in heaven. When they were heathen, they used to kill almost all their children when they were small; and many of them were murdered, and given to their idol gods. One day, when the little church there was sitting down at the communion table, a poor woman, who had been a heathen, but who was now a Christian, was seen to weep most bitterly. One of the ministers asked her why she wept and wrung her hands. "Oh!" said she, "why did I not know of this blessed God before! Why did I not! I once had six sweet children—they are all gone—I murdered them all with my own hands! But oh, if I had known about God as I now do, they would have been alive now!" They have now done with the cruel practice of murdering their children. They know better.

Perhaps some of my little hearers are orphans,—have no father, or no mother. I can feel for such; for I know what it is to stand by the grave of a father when a child.[27]

---

[27] Dr. Todd's father was a physician in Rutland, Vermont when he was severely injured rushing to the aid of a dying man. Although he recovered, and did not lose his leg, he later died and left young John fatherless at six years of age.

But let me say to you, that God will take care of you. He takes care of the lily. You have heard of the ostrich, that great bird which lives in the wilderness. She lays her eggs in the sand, and then leaves them forever. The warm sun hatches out the young ostrich, and there is no mother to feed and take care of it. But God takes care of it, and feeds it; and will he not much more take care of the child who has lost father or mother, if that child ask him to be a father? Surely he will!

Children, you have all yet to meet with trials and disappointments. You are meeting with them every day. You will have sickness, and pain, and sorrow, and you need a friend whose love cannot change. You must die, and be buried up in the ground; and you want God to take care of you, whether you live in this world or in the next. Well, God will be such a friend to you on these conditions:

You must ask him to be your father and friend. Ask him every day, and feel that without his blessing upon you every day, your feet may fall, your eyes fill with tears, and your soul meet with death. Ask in the name of Jesus Christ.

You must promise him sincerely that you will obey him and do his will. Suppose you had no father or no mother, and a great, and good, and rich man were to offer to take you, and take care of you, and make you his own child, and should say he would do it all, on the condition that you obliged him and did his will,—would you not at once promise to do it? And so you ought to promise God.

You must love God as you would the best father in the world. Love his Son, because he is the express image of the Father.[28] Love his word, his people, his service, his commands, his duties, and thus give him your heart, and he will be your friend forever and ever. Amen.

---

[28] Hebrews 1:3.

LECTURE VII

JESUS CHRIST TASTING DEATH

Jesus—who, by the grace of God,
should taste death for every man. –Heb. 2:9

Figurative language. Fields smiling. The sea afraid. Meaning of the text. How they used to put people to death. Socrates' death. Long row of prisoners. Christ drinking the cup of poison. Children of Israel. The court-house. The young prisoner. His plea. His home. His family. The parting. Killing his parents. The compassionate judge. The pardon. Christ died for us. All saved? The hospital. The house for all the blind. Offered to all. A question answered. Light for all. Water for all. Salvation of Christ free. A thing to be remembered. The story of the slave. The good man. The slave bought. Ingratitude. All men slaves. John Howard. Four things to be done.

If I should speak about *figurative* language, I wonder if these children would know what I mean? Some, no doubt, would. But lest all could not understand it, I will tell you what I mean. If I should walk out with one of these children, on some fair and beautiful morning, and see the bright sun, and the trees full of blossoms, and the ground covered with green grass, and hear the birds sing, I might stop and say to my little friend, "How pleasant! The very fields *smile!*" By this I should not mean that the fields have eyes, and a mouth, and a face, and can smile, just as we do. But this is figurative language. So when the Bible says, "The sea saw God, and was afraid,"[29] it means the waters rolled back, and went away, just as a man would run away when he was afraid. This is figurative language. The sea

---

[29] Dr. Todd is alluding to Psalm 114:3.

rolled back, just as if it were afraid. The fields look pleasant, just as a man does when he smiles.

Now, see if you cannot understand this beautiful text.[30] In the times when the Bible was written, they used to put men to death, who had broken the laws, in different ways. Some were stoned to death. Some were drowned. But one very common way was, to make them take a cup and drink what was in it. This cup used to have poison in it. The condemned man drank it, and in a few moments was dead. In this way Socrates,[31] one of the best heathen that ever lived, and put to death unjustly, died. "The fatal cup was brought. Socrates asked what was necessary for him to do. 'Nothing more,' replied the servant, 'than, as soon as you have drank it, to walk about till you find your legs grow weary, and afterwards lie down upon your bed.' He took up the cup without any emotion or change in his color or countenance—and then drank down the whole draught with an amazing tranquility."

Now, this text represents all men as guilty of crime, and justly condemned to die. It is just as if all were shut up in prison, and doomed to drink, each a cup full of poison. Just suppose the prison doors to be opened, and the poor men all brought out and placed in a long row, and each man holding a cup of poison in his hand, which he must drink. Then, at that moment, Jesus Christ comes along, and pities the poor guilty prisoners, and goes slowly along, takes each cup out of the hand, and drinks it himself! This is drinking, or "tasting death for every man!" This is just as if Christ had done so for sinners. This is figurative language; but you now understand it; and whenever you read over this delightful text, you will know it means, that Christ died for sinners, and thus saved them from hell, just as he would save the poor prisoners, if he should drink the cup of poison for each one!

---

[30] Hebrews 2:9.
[31] Socrates lived from 469-399 BC.

You know how mercies may come to people sometimes, not on their own account, but on the account of others. To make this plain:—the children of Israel all sinned against God in the wilderness, and God was about to kill them all. But Moses went and prayed for them; and God heard his prayers, and spared the wicked Hebrews for the sake of Moses. When Joseph was sold a slave in Egypt, God blessed his master, and blessed all Egypt, for the sake of Joseph. And men who are guilty, and who deserve to die, can sometimes be forgiven for the sake of others, who are not guilty. This I will try to make plain to you.

Suppose, in one of your walks, you go into the court-house, while the court are doing their business. You go in, and find the great room full of people. A young man has just been tried for committing an awful crime. The lawyers have done pleading for him, and he is proved to be guilty. He must die; and he has now been brought into the court to hear the sentence of death. The judge rises up with a paper in his hand, on which the sentence is written. He looks towards the young man, and says,

"Young man, the court has found you guilty. Is there any reason why the sentence of death should not now be pronounced upon you?"

The young man rises up. His hands are clasped together in agony. The sheriff stands close by him, so that he shall not escape. He stands a moment, and the tears fall fast from his cheeks. He falters,—and then speaks:

"Sir, I have to thank you for the kind manner in which I have been tried. I deserve to die, and, for myself, I cannot, and I do not, ask for life. But, sir, far away from this, in a remote corner of the country, there is a high mountain rising up towards heaven. At the foot of that mountain is a beautiful meadow, with a sweet little brook winding through it. On the banks of that brook, and just at the foot of the mountain, stands a little cottage, under the lofty elms that hang over it. And there I spent my boyhood. The stream was never dry, and the meadows were always green. There I lived, happy as the lark which flew over my head.

In that little cottage there lives an old, worn-out soldier, who fought and bled for his country. You can remember how you and he fought side by side, and how he once saved the life of his general, at the risk of his own. He is an old man;—his hair is gray;—he leans upon a staff when he walks. And beside him sits a feeble woman. They are my father and my mother. At their feet sit my two little sisters, who, every night, go to the little window, and stand and watch as long as they can see, in hopes to see me return. For, when I left my home, and my father laid his hand on my head, and prayed for me, and my mother wept her blessing over me, and my sisters hung upon my arm, I promised to return again, and be the comfort, the stay, and the staff of that family. And now, sir, when I am gone,—when I am cut off with all the sins of my youth fresh upon me,—the tidings will all go to that distant cottage, and the news will kill that old man, my father, and that aged woman, my mother. Yes, they will sink down in sorrow to the grave; and my orphan sisters will be turned out upon a world whose charities will be cold towards the sisters of one who died on the gallows. Oh, sir, how can I die, and bury that family in ruin! Oh, save me, for the sake of that old soldier, who shed his blood freely for his country, and that mother, whose prayers will cover your head as long as she lives, and those sisters, who will never lie down without praying for you! For *my* sake, I dare not ask life; but for *their* sakes, I ask and entreat it!"

The humane judge is moved; he is a father, and he weeps. He says, "Young man, I cannot pardon you. I must pass the sentence of the law upon you. But I will commend you to the governor, who has the power to pardon you. I will tell him your story, and I hope, for the *sake* of that old soldier, your father, he will pardon you; but till his mind is known, you are condemned."

Now follow the good judge. He goes to the governor. He states the case, the crime, the guilt of the youth. He also states the situation of the old father whose only son is condemned to the gallows. The governor listens. His heart, too, is moved, and he pardons the young man, and sends him home, not because *he* deserved pardon, but for the sake of his father's family. This, now, is a plain case, where a man may receive pardon for the sake of another. Just so, for the sake of Jesus Christ, men may be pardoned by God, and prepared for heaven. In this way have more good people gone to heaven than we could count—a multitude from every nation under heaven.[32]

But perhaps I should here ask you a question. If Christ died for all men, tasted death for every man, will every man, of course, go to heaven? I answer, No; not of course. Let me show you how it is. At Boston they have built a great and a

---

[32] Revelation 7:9.

beautiful house for sick people to be carried to, in order to be taken care of, and cured. It is called a hospital. It is built for the use of every man in Massachusetts—if he chooses to go to it. It is so that any person who wishes may go there and enjoy its accommodations. Now, if anybody does not feel sick, he need not go there. He may be sick at home, if he chooses. Still he has a right to go to the hospital. It was built for everybody. So Christ died for all men, and is ready to save all men; but if any do not feel their need of him, or if they choose to go somewhere else for pardon, they can, and, of course, they are not saved by Christ.

Suppose I am a rich man, and I build a great house, and call it the house for blind people; and print it in all the newspapers, that the house is all ready and complete, and that every blind child in the land may come and live in it; that I will give him food and clothing, will have him instructed, and will even cure him of his blindness. But I have one condition; and that is, that all the blind children who come shall behave well, and be good children, and obey all the rules of the house. This would be a house for all the blind in the land. But would all come to it? No. Some would say, they do not wish to be fed and clothed. Some would say, they do not wish to be taught. And some would say, they do not wish to be cured; they had as gladly be blind as not. And thus there might be multitudes who are blind, but who receive no good from my house. Just so with men in regard to Jesus Christ. All may go to him and be saved; but all will not choose to go; and none will be saved except those who do go to him, and who obey him.

But will God, perhaps you ask, provide for all, and yet all not receive salvation? Will he lay a foundation for a great church, and yet set only a small building on it? I reply to you, that God has provided a Savior, who is able and willing to save all men; and yet he will save none but those who break off from sin, and obey him. What child needs to have me tell him that God provides many blessings which all do not enjoy, though all might, if they chose? He has created sunshine enough for all. But some are so wicked that they had rather be thieves, and go to steal in the night, and sleep when the sun shines. Still there is light enough for all, if all choose to use it. So, also, God has created water enough to supply every thirsty man on earth; but some choose not to drink it; they had rather drink some strong drink, which destroys them. But there is water enough, and it is their fault if they do not use it. Does any man ever say that God could not and did not write the Bible? or that God has not appointed and blessed the holy Sabbath, because so many people choose to break the Sabbath, and waste it? No. In all these cases, we know that God has, in mercy, provided these blessings, and then left men to do as they please about enjoying them.

It is just so with the salvation by Jesus Christ. It is as free as the water which flows from the clouds; but, then, men may do as they please about going to Christ for it. He healed every sick man who came to him, when he was on earth; but if any were sick, and did not go to him, or send to him, such he did not heal.

I have almost done this Lecture. But I want to say a word more to these dear children, and to say, if I can, such a thing, and in such a manner, that they will not forget it. What I wish to say is this, *that it is very wrong not to love Jesus Christ for his mercy in tasting death for every man.*

Now, suppose I should say to you, "Children, I am now going to tell you a story about myself; and the story is this. Just suppose it true. I was once out on the great waters, far out upon the ocean, in a large ship, going to the Indies. On one fine morning, another ship came in sight, and bent her course so as to come straight towards us. We were afraid of her, and so we hoisted up every sail we could, in order to get away. But she gained upon us, and we could not escape. So she sailed up to us, a great ship, full of men, and guns, and swords. They took us all, and carried us to their country, and put irons on our hands and on our feet, and stripped off our clothes, and sold us in the market for slaves, just as they would cattle. I was bought by a cruel, wicked man, who almost starved me, and who used to whip me every day till the blood ran down my back. So I lived for years. The news at length reached my native place. And then the richest and the best man in the whole country, and one whom I had always treated unkindly, heard of my condition. He felt for me. At once he sold his house, his lands, and everything he had, and took all he had in the world, and went into that distant country, to buy me out of slavery. When he got there, he told what he wanted. My master would not sell me. The good man offered all his money, and to become poor himself. No,—my master would not take it. At last, the good man offered to become a slave himself, if I might be set at liberty. The offer was accepted. I had the irons taken off from my hands, and put on his; and the stripes which I had received, were laid upon him. I saw him a poor slave, and knew that he had left home and friends, and had become a slave, to buy my freedom! I came home to my friends, where I have a home and so many blessings. And now I forget that friend who became a slave in my place. I never speak of him; I never write to him, never thank him; never have tried to love him or his friends! Is not this ungrateful? Is it not wrong, and sinful? And have I not got a very wicked heart?"

Now, just see how this applies to us. We were all taken and made slaves by sin. We were all in bondage, and all ruined. Jesus Christ was in heaven, with the Father. His eye pitied us. He was rich, and had all in heaven for his own; but he became a poor man. For our sakes, he became poor.[33] He came, like an angel, on the wings of love, down to this world, where we poor slaves live. He would buy us. And he bought us by becoming a curse for

---

[33] 2 Corinthians 8:9.

69

us; bought us, "not with corruptible things, as with silver and gold," but by his own precious blood.[34] "The Lord hath laid on him the iniquity of us all, and by his stripes we are healed."[35] Ought we not to love Jesus Christ, and that, too, with all the heart?

Christ died for us while we were enemies.[36] The great and the good John Howard[37] went all over Europe to visit the prisons and to do good to the poor prisoners. When he entered a prison, the prisoners would frequently go the whole length of their chain, to fall at his feet and bless him. But they were not his enemies, nor did he die for them. But Christ died for us, while we were enemies. What a love is this! What a Savior is he! "What think ye of Christ,"[38] my dear children? Should you not at once begin to do, and continue to do, these four things?

1.   Think about Jesus Christ every day, in your own heart.

2.   Read about Christ in the Bible, and try to know as much about him as you possibly can.

3.   Think how little you have thought of him, or cared for him, and be humbled and truly sorry.

4.   Give him your love, your heart, your life, your all. Amen.

---

[34] 1 Peter 1:18,19.
[35] Isaiah 53:5,6.
[36] Romans 5:10.
[37] John Howard (1726-1790), known simply as *The Philanthropist*, devoted his life to minister to those in deepest misery, especially in the prisons.
[38] Matthew 22:42.

LECTURE VIII

CHRIST INTERCEDING FOR US

"He ever liveth to make intercession." – Heb.7:25

The name of Washington. We all want a friend. The poor Indian and his child. Christ is such a friend as we need. Children's troubles. The three friends. The real friend. Story applied. Christ is the real friend. When most needed. The just king and his laws. Christ's manner of interceding. High treason. The wife and ten children. The pardon. How is Christ's intercession different? The child in prison. The two brothers. Four things in Christ. He is worthy. He knows our wants. He ever lives. He never changes. The waters quench not his love.

Almost every prayer which we hear is made in the name of Jesus Christ; and everything we ask God for, is asked "for Christ's sake." A poor, sick soldier might go to the door of congress, and ask to go in, and ask for help for himself and his family, and he could not get any. But if he had in his pocket a paper, saying that he might go and ask help in the name of Washington, and if congress knew that the paper was written by Washington, they would hear his request, and aid him, for Washington's sake. This would be asking in another's name, just as we ask God in Christ's name; and it would be answering for another's sake, just as God answers us "for Christ's sake."[39]

Nobody can feel happy without a friend. And almost every one tries to get and keep a few friends, however wicked he may be. Let any one have no friend to feel for him, to share his joys and his sorrows, and he will feel unhappy. You

---

[39] Romans 15:30; 1 Corinthians 4:10; 2 Corinthians 12:10; Ephesians 4:32.

have seen how children will love a little dog, or a lamb, or a dove, or anything that can love them. The little boy will talk to his top, and the little girl will talk to her doll, because they want a friend; and if the top and the doll could talk, and love them, they would be still more glad. Why? Because we all want friends, to whom we can talk, and who will feel for us. Let me show you just what I mean.

Some years ago, there was an Indian in the state of Maine, who, for his very good conduct, had a large farm given him by the state. He built his little house on his land, and there lived. Around him were quite a number of white families. They did not treat him badly, but, because he was an Indian, they did not act and feel as if they loved him, and as if they were his friends. His only child was taken sick, and died, and not one of the white people went near him to comfort him, or to aid him to bury his little child. A few days after, he came to the white people, and said to them,

"When white man's child die, Indian man be sorry,—he help bury him. When my child die, no one speak to me—I make his grave alone,—I can't live here,—and have no friend to love me!"

The poor Indian gave up his farm, *dug up the body of his child, and carried it with him two hundred miles through the forest,* to join the Canada Indians! What love for his child! What a deep feeling in his heart, that he wanted a friend!

So we all want some one to whom we may look every day. But when we are sick, when in distress, when we are about to die, oh, then, we want a friend who will stand near us, and who can help us. Now, Jesus Christ is just that friend. He was once a man of sorrows, and was acquainted with grief, and knows how to help those who are in sorrow.[40] He was once in the agonies of death, and knows all how the dying feel. Is any one poor? So was he,

---

[40] Isaiah 53:3.

and knows all about being poor. Are you a poor weak child? So was he, and knows just how the child feels, and just what a friend he needs. You have little trials and troubles, which older people would not think of, but which sometimes make your heart feel heavy and sad. Well, Jesus Christ knows all about such feelings, and can help you, and will do it every day, if you ask him every day to do so.

But though we want a friend all our lives, there is one hour when we very much need such a friend. That is the hour of dying. Let me show you why.

There was once a man who had three friends. He knew them, and lived near them for years. It so happened, that this man was accused to the king of the country as a bad man, and the king ordered that he should be put to death. The poor man heard of it, and was in great trouble. He expected to lose his life, and to leave his family of children in great distress. After thinking it over, and weeping over it, he determined to go to the king, and fall down before him, and get somebody to go with him, and beg his life. So he called on these three friends, and begged them to go with him. The first whom he asked, he loved best, and thought him his best friend. But no;—he would not go with him one step towards the king's court. He would not move to help him. He next went to the second friend, and whom he loved next best, and asked him to go. So they set out to go; but when they came to the gates of the king's court, this friend stopped, and would not go in with him, and ask for his life. Then he went to the third friend, and the one whom he loved the least, and asked him to help him. This friend was known to the king, and beloved *by* him. So he took him by the hand, and led him in to the king, and *interceded,* or begged for him, and the king pardoned the condemned man, *for the sake of his friend who interceded for him!*

Now, see how this story applies here. People have three things, which they think of, and which they call their friends. These three things are, 1. The world; that is, property, and houses, and all the fine things which they have. 2. Their friends. 3. Jesus Christ. The first of these friends is loved the most. Our friends are loved next best; and Jesus Christ least of all. So, when we are taken sick, and must die, and go in before the great King, we call upon these to help us. The world, and the things of the world, however, cannot go with us one step. They must all be useless the moment we lie on the bed of death. The next, which is, our friends, can go with us through the sickness, and as far as to the king's gates, the gates of death, and they there stop and leave us. But Jesus Christ, that friend, of whom we think so little, and whom we love so little, he can go in with us before the great King of kings, and plead for us, *intercede* for us, and thus save our souls from being condemned to eternal death. This, oh, *this* is the time when we need him for our friend, and need him for our intercessor. He died for us, and can, therefore, be our friend, and plead for us, and save us.

I trust you have not forgotten the last Lecture, in which I tried to show you how that God can save our souls, because Christ suffered for us. I am now showing you that Christ does something more; he intercedes for us. A king once made a law against a certain crime; and the law was, that every one who did that wicked thing should have both his eyes put out. Very soon, a man was found who had broken the law. He was tried and found guilty. It was the king's own son. Now, the king saw that, if he did not punish his son, nobody ought to be punished, and nobody would keep the law. So he had one eye of his son put out, and one of his own eyes put out! He could now go before the court and plead for his son, and, by his own sufferings and intercession, could save his son from further punishment. All the people saw that the good king hated the crime and loved his laws. Just so does Jesus Christ save us. He has suffered for us, and now lives to intercede for us.[41]

How very different are Christ's prayers for us from anything which we can do for one another! He can always aid us. We cannot always do it. Let me try to show you the difference.

Many years ago, there were some men, in the state of Pennsylvania, who would not obey the laws of their country, but tried to destroy the laws, and have their own wills. When men go so far as to unite, and say they will not obey the laws, this crime is called "high treason." Among these men who did so, was one by the name of John Fries.[42] He was carefully tried by the court, and found guilty, and sentenced to be hung. The death-warrant was signed by the president of the United States, and the day was fixed on which he should die. But just before the day came, some people went to the president, and asked him to permit a woman to see him, who had something to say to him. The president said he would see her. A few kind friends went with her to the house of the president. The president stood up to receive her. But what was his surprise to see this woman with ten children all kneeling before him in tears! They were the wife and the ten children of John Fries, kneeling and weeping, and *interceding* for the life of their father, who was condemned to die! The president stood in amazement; and then the big tears came gushing down his cheeks, and his voice was so choked, that he could not speak. With his eyes streaming with tears, and his hands raised towards heaven, he pushed away out of the room. Oh, what a moment of anxiety!

---

[41] Hebrews 7:25.

[42] The president was John Adams, and the entire account is discussed in the book *Fries's Rebellion: The Enduring Struggle for the American Revolution* by Paul Douglas Newman, published by University of Pennsylvania Press.

Would he hear the petition, or would he let the man die? In a few moments he returned with a paper in his hand. It contained a full and free pardon for her husband, and their father. He gave it to Mrs. Fries, and she went away, and returned joyful to her home, having her husband with her.

This was interceding before a human being. Christ intercedes before God. This was interceding for one man. Christ does it for all his people. This was for one short life. Christ asks for us eternal life. This was for one sin. Christ intercedes for all our sins. This was for a friend. Christ does it for those who have ever been his enemies. This saved from the curse pronounced by human laws. Christ saves us from the curse of God's law. This was a little stream; but Christ carries us over the dark river of death.

Suppose one of these children were condemned to die, and were shut up in prison, and were going to send a petition to the governor for your life. Whom would you wish to carry it? The most worthy man in the whole town, certainly. Christ is the most worthy being in the universe, and therefore he is a good intercessor. If you were to petition for your life, whom would you wish to carry your petition; a stranger, or some warm, intimate friend of the governor? The friend, surely. You would say, the governor will be more likely to hear his friend than a stranger. Yes. And God is ever well-pleased with his dear Son, and is willing to hear him when he intercedes for us.

History informs us of a man who was doomed to die for some crime which he had committed. His brother had lost an arm in defending his country. He came forward and held up the stump of his lost arm, and interceded for his brother. The judges were so affected by the remembrance of his past services that they freely pardoned the guilty brother for his sake. Thus is Christ described to us as sitting on the throne, with his wounds yet bleeding (Revelation 5:6) and interceding for us.

Lecture Eight: *Christ Interceding For Us*

There are four things about Jesus Christ which make him just such an intercessor as we need. I will tell you what they are.

1. *He is worthy.* You know, dear children, that it is a great comfort to have good men pray for us. You know, too, that the prayers of good men avail much with God. In the Bible you will find the stories, where one man prayed, and the dead child of a heathen woman was raised to life; where another prayed, and an angel came down and shut the mouths of lions, so that they did not hurt the good man. Peter prayed, and a dead woman came to life. Paul prayed, and a young man, who had fallen from the third story of the house, and was killed, was brought to life. Abraham prayed for Sodom and Gomorrah, and the cities would have been spared, if there had been ten righteous men in five cities. But good men might pray for you; all the good men on earth might, and if Christ should not also, it would not do you any good. No. And all the good spirits in heaven, saints and angels, even up to Gabriel, might pray for you, and all would not be so good as one prayer of Christ. He is worthy. The saints and the angels cast their crowns at his feet, and cry, "Thou art worthy." He is worshipped by all in heaven. He sits on the throne with God, and God loves him, and will hear him in our behalf.

2. *Christ knows your wants.* I sometimes pray with these children, and for them. I shall do so again when this Lecture is done. But it is some years since I was a child; and I forget how a child feels, and what his wants are. So does every man. Were David to pray for you, he would forget how he used to feel when a child. So would Abraham, so would all heaven. Not so with Jesus Christ. He never forgets how he felt when he was a child. He can look at once down on the heart, and knows every feeling, every fear, every sorrow, every want. You can conceal nothing from his eye. And when he intercedes for you, he knows exactly what you need. He knows better than your mother, and even better than you know yourself.

77

3. *Christ will ever live to intercede for you.* Good parents may pray for you often. So may good ministers. But they cannot do it long. They must soon die, and leave you. They will soon all be gone. But Christ is alive today; he will be alive tomorrow; he will be alive when you come to die, and your soul goes into the eternal world. And when the graves are opened, when the sun goes down to rise no more, and the moon and the stars all fade away, he will still live, and live to intercede for his disciples. Death will take us all away, but *he* dies no more.

4. *Christ never changes.* Almost everything changes. The weather changes, the trees change, the flowers change, and all things which we see. Friends also change. Some go away from us. Some are good friends when we are well, but leave us when we are in trouble. The severe lines of the poet are often true:

"The friends, who in our sunshine-live,
    When winter comes, are flown;
And he who hast but tears to give,
    Must weep those tears alone."[43]

Yes, we may all change; we may be disappointed, may be in sorrow, may be in sickness, may be in the agonies of death; but Christ never changes, never leaves us, never forgets us. We may sink into the cold, swelling river, and be drowning, and our friends stand on the banks, not daring to go in after us; but his love cannot be quenched by the cold waters of "many floods." We shall die, and our bodies sleep in the grave. We shall awake again at the resurrection day. But in all this Christ does not change. "The same yesterday, today, and forever,"[44] he ever liveth to intercede for us. O what a Redeemer! "Blessed, O Lord, is the man who trusteth in thee."[45] Amen.

---

[43] Taken from a poem by Thomas Moore (1779-1852).
[44] Hebrews 13:8.
[45] Psalm 34:8; 84:12.

LECTURE IX

GIVING ACCOUNT TO GOD

"Every one of us shall give account of himself to God." – Rom.14:12

Plain text. The stranger. His account of himself.How different from the account to God. The merchant. Account of one of these boys. Fields, horses and plants called to account. The plant producing no flower. How a father feels. The house burned. The soul poisoned. The father's feelings over a murdered child. Every one must give account. How can children sin? How much does a child sin? The little rattlesnake. What murder is. Anger. The Bible destroyed. The bones broken. The Sabbath lost. The child killing people. Conscience. The fruit-trees. The broken bowl. Three directions. The Roman emperor.

This seems to he one of the plainest texts in the Bible. It tells you *who* shall give an account; "every one of us." It tells us *to whom* you shall give an account; "to God;" and *about whom* you must give the account; "of himself." So far is plain. But perhaps these children will mistake, after all. Let me make it so plain that you cannot mistake it. Suppose, when you go home tonight, a stranger comes into your house, and is asked to stay and spend the evening. He is very pleasant, and talks with all the family; and, among others, he talks with the children. He tells them he has been away off on the great waters, in a ship, to catch whales; that, one day, when trying to kill a poor whale, the wounded fish turned and struck the ship with his tail, and broke it all in pieces; that he and his few men who were not drowned, got into a little boat, and rowed off, day and night, for many days, till nearly all were dead,—starved to death;—that they were then cast upon a low, desert island, where they lived upon fish, and such things, for years, till a ship happened to pass that way, and took them, and brought them home. Thus he tells you the whole *account* of his life. You thank him for it. It is an interesting and useful account. You love to hear it. But this is not what is meant by giving account to God. *Why* not? Because he is not obliged to give the account to you, unless he pleases; but we *must* do it to God. Because, also, you cannot know whether or not it is the *true* account of his life; but God will know whether we give a true account or not. Because, too, you could not reward him for the times when he did well, nor punish him when he did wrong; but when we give account to God, he will reward us, or punish us, as we have done right or wrong.

A merchant might tell us all about his bargains, his ships, his losses, and gains, and the curious things with which he has met; but though the account of his life is very interesting, yet it is not such an account as we must give to God. A lawyer could give you an account of what he has seen,—what prisoners tried for stealing,—others for murder,—and how the friends were present, and how they seemed to be broken-hearted when the sentence of death was pronounced; but this is not such an account as we must give to God at last.

Suppose that one of those little boys in that front seat should now get up, and try to give me an account of his whole life. Could he do it in such a way as he would have to, if God should call him to do it? No. Because he would not be likely to remember but a small part of it; and I could not know the rest, as God can. He would not feel willing to put into the account all the foolish and wicked words he has ever said; the wicked thoughts and feelings he has ever had; nor the wrong things he has ever done. And I could not tell them. Besides, I could not know how to punish or reward him as he deserves; but God knows just how to do it. I should have no right to do it, if I could; but God would have the right. So you see, that it is a very different thing to give an account to God from what it would be to give it to a man.

We call almost everything to account in some way or other. Just see. Did you never see a farmer go out and look carefully at the waving wheat in the field, and, taking some of the wheat-heads in his hand, rub them to get the wheat out? Why was he doing it? To see if it had much wheat in it, and to see if it were good, full wheat. This was a kind of trial, or account, to which he was calling his wheat. When a man buys a new watch or clock, you will see him examining it every day, and looking carefully to see if it goes, and goes right. Yes, he calls it to account; and if it goes wrong, or stops, he sends it back, and will not keep it. And he would blame it severely, if it could understand him, and knew better.

Let a man own a horse, and keep him, and take good care of him, and he will blame the horse, and whip him, if he is not kind, and does not obey him. The very horse is called to an account for his conduct. Yes, if one of these little girls had a plant, which she had kept, and watered, and taken care of for years, and if it never produced one single blossom, she would feel discouraged, and call it to an account, and give it up, and let it perish. She would call the frail plant to a kind of account, and treat it according to its character. She might grieve over her plant, and even shed tears to have it turn out so poorly; but she would not keep taking care of it, if it were a useless plant, and never blossomed.

Some seem to think that God does not care how we live in this world. But let us see. In the Bible, he is called our Father. Does a father love to see a child do wrong? Suppose the father of one of you should go away on a journey, and should hear, while gone, that a wicked man had set his barn on fire, and burned up all his hay and his cattle. Would he not feel as if the wicked man ought to be called to an account? Suppose, the next day, he should hear that the same wicked man had set his house on fire, and had burned it to ashes, and, in doing this, had burned up one of his dear children. Would he not feel grieved? Would he not think the wicked man ought to be called to account, and punished? Yes, he would. Well, do you not suppose our Father in heaven feels just so towards those who sin, and do wrong? Suppose I should give one of these dear children poison, and should tell him it was food, and he should believe me, and it should kill him. Ought I not to be called to account, and punished? Certainly I had. But suppose I should, by any means, poison the mind, and tell you what is not true, and make you lose your soul forever. Ought I not to be called to account? Yes, I ought to be. But nobody can do it but God, and he will do it.

Now, suppose, as you go home, and as you get away at some distance, you see an old man, with gray hair, bending over and leaning on his staff. He is looking down towards the ground. As you get near him, you see blood on the ground; and you see a little girl lying and bleeding in the path just before the old man. She is pale; her eyes are closed; and the blood runs out of her mouth and ears; and she is dead. She moves no more than the stones. She has been murdered. But who is that old man bending over her? Oh! he is her father,—and she is his youngest child. She was walking with him, and clinging to his arm, when a wicked man came up, and struck her with a club, and, in spite of the cries and entreaties of her father, kept striking, till she was dead! What think you? Does not that old man's heart ache? Does not that good father wish to have the murderer called to an account and punished? Yes, he does. He cannot but wish so. And so does our Father in heaven feel when he sees sin. It may be only anger in the heart; but he sees it so clearly that it is murder in his sight. And so he will call us to an account. God can no more look upon sin without disliking it, than a father can see his children murdered, without wishing the man who does it to be called to an account.

Every child knows that every man must give account of his conduct to somebody. The child must give account to his parents and to his teachers. The teacher must give a kind of account to the parents. The parents must give account to conscience, to society around, and to God. But has the child much of an account to give to God? Let us see.

Take one of these children who is eight years old. That child has had fifty-two Sabbaths every year, for eight years: this is over four hundred Sabbaths. Has he kept all these Sabbaths holy? Has no one of them been lost, and wasted? All these have been seasons of mercy, in which he might learn about God, and Christ, and heaven. But there are three hundred and sixty-five days in every year; and so that child has lived almost three thousand days. In each day, how many times has he thought of God? In each day, he could disobey his parents more than once;

speak cross and wicked words more than once; neglect to pray to God more than once, and have many wicked thoughts and feelings in his heart. Oh, how many days has that child lived and hardly thought of God! And yet, every day, God has awaked him in the morning, and fed him with food, and clothed him, and kept him alive. When he has been sick, God came to the bed-side and cured him. When he was in danger of dying, God has made him well; and all these many days, God has been doing good to him. Say, has not that child a great account to give to God?

Some people seem to feel that *a child* does not commit sin; or, if he does, his sins are few, and very small. But I hope you will not feel so, till you have thought much upon it. I will examine it for a few moments. All know that it is wrong to be angry. God declares that anger in the heart is murder. It may not seem to be murder to you. Now, does the little beautiful snake, not longer than your finger, seem to be a very bad creature? But keep him, and feed him, and let him grow; and you will soon see him turning red on the back, and hear him hiss with his tongue; and he is soon the deadly rattlesnake, who, with a single bite, can kill any body. Just so with anger. If it dies away in the heart, nobody but God knows it. If it swells still larger, it breaks out in cross looks, and cross words, and perhaps makes the hand strike. If it swells still larger, it may raise the arm, and stab, and kill. The arm does not move of itself. No, it is the wicked feelings within which move it to kill.

Now, suppose a dollar in money must be paid for every time these children have ever been angry in all their lives. Who would be able to pay it? If not one of them could be saved, unless a dollar was paid for each angry feeling which he has ever had, who could buy his salvation? who would engage to do it?

Suppose there were now only one Bible in the world, and that one is this lying on the pulpit before me. From this one, all the Bibles which the world are ever to have, must be copied. And suppose God should now speak from heaven, and say, "This Bible must lie here one year without being moved; and every time one of these children commits a single sin, one page of the Bible shall drop out and perish forever!" Pray tell me, if many, many pages would not be gone before the year is out? Tell me, if what was left would not be a very poor Bible? And will any body say that children do not sin?

Suppose, too, that God should say, "I will now pardon all the sins which these children have ever committed; all shall be forgiven; but every child who sins after this, shall have one of his bones broken for every sin which he ever commits!" Do you not think that one and another would soon be cripples? What child here would live a month or a week without having some bones broken? And will any one say that children do not sin?

If God should say, "Take the best child in this house, and let him hear what I am to say; every time you break the Sabbath, one Sabbath shall forever be taken away out of each year!" How long would it take that child to sin away all our Sabbaths? Do not children sin?

Once more. Suppose that one of these children be called out from the rest,—no matter which one it is,—but one be called out, to stand up in the aisle there, and God should say, "For the first sin, and for every sin, which that child commits, the person who is nearest to him shall drop down dead;—and so on, as long as he lives, every sin shall kill the person who is nearest to him!" Who would not fear? Why, every one in this house would flee out for his life; every one would run for the door, so as not to be the nearest person. And before we all got out, a sin would rise up in his heart, and one would drop down dead, and then another, and perhaps another! Oh, what a terror would that child be! The angel of death, on his pale horse, could not be more feared. And, now, will any one say that children do not sin? And have they not a great account to give to God?

There is another way by which you may know whether or not you are sinners; and that is, by asking your own hearts. Let the boys of a family be at play together on a mild afternoon. Their father tells them they must be careful and do no mischief. But, when he comes home at night, he finds some one has cut, and mangled, and killed several of his young fruit-trees. One of his boys has done it. He calls them to an account. Now, who is afraid to be called to the account? Most plainly, the boy who has done the mischief. The rest are not afraid. So with you. No child would be afraid of God, were it not that the heart tells him that he is a sinner. A mother comes into the room where her little daughters have been playing. She finds the cupboard door open, and her sugar-bowl all broken in pieces. Which of the little girls is now afraid? Why, the one who has done the mischief. And all, who are afraid of God, are afraid because they are sinners. And all are sinners. Oh, that God would make us holy!

Let me close this Lecture with three short directions.

1. *Every day be careful how you live—because you must give account to God for every day.* Do nothing of which you will feel ashamed when God calls you to account. Omit no duty which God tells you to do. You will be sorry for every sin when you come to die.

2. *Learn something of God every day.* You may learn about God by thinking of him, talking about him, reading about him, and praying to him. The more you know about God, the more you will fear to sin, and the more you will try to please him.

3. *Do something every day which will please God, and which will make you glad in the great day of accounts.* Titus, a heathen emperor, through all his life used to call himself to account, every night, for the actions of the day past; and when one day had slipped without his doing some good, he used to write, "I have lost a day." He did not know of a judgment-day; but you do; and therefore lose no day, in which you do not something and much to please God. Amen.

LECTURE X

GREAT EVENTS HANG ON LITTLE THINGS

"A certain man drew a bow at a venture." – 1 Kings 22:34

The man and his bow and arrow. What an arrow can do. The subject stated. The ship-yard. The wormy stick. The leaky ship. The result. The child and the acorn. The oak. The result. The light-house removed. A little mistake. Ship and lives lost. Result. Great fires in the forest. Little boy playing with fire. The spark caught. The mother of Mohammed. The consequence. How it is with these children. What the subject teaches. The child did not tell a lie. The tongue. Company. Every day. The little stream. The last thing taught by this subject.

This chapter gives an account of a war between two kingdoms. They were the kingdoms of Israel and of Syria. They fought hard, and shed much blood. Ahab was king of Israel. When going out on the battle-field, he put off his kingly dress, and put on such clothes as other men wear, lest they should know him and should kill him. During the battle, a man (but what his name was, or what his history was, we know not)—a man held his bow and arrow in his hand. He thought he would shoot towards the army of Israel. He saw no man at whom he especially desired to aim. Perhaps he paused a moment, and doubted whether he should shoot or not. But the arrow was in his hand, and he put it to the string of his bow. Now, is it any matter whether he shoots or not? He raises the bow to shoot. Is it any matter whether he shoots one way or another? Yes; much depends upon his shooting, and which way he takes aim with his arrow. He shoots,—the arrow flies,—the wind does not turn it aside out of the way,—it goes towards a chariot. The harness, at that moment, just opens a little at the joints. There, now! it goes in at that little opening. Hark! there is a groan. It has hit the king; it has killed the king! Ahab, the great king, who built great cities, and built an ivory horse, and who carried on great wars, is killed, and the war is put to an end, by that little arrow, which any one of these children could have broken with the fingers in a moment! Oh, how much sometimes hangs on little things!

And this is just what I am wishing to show to these children; *that great results do often hang on little things.*

Two men were at work together one day in a ship-yard. They were hewing a stick of timber to put into a ship. It was a small stick, and not worth much. As they cut off the chips, they found a worm, a little worm, about half an inch long.

"This stick is wormy," said one; "shall we put it in?"

"I do not know; yes, I think it may go in. It will never be seen, of course."

"Yes, but there may be other worms in it; and these may increase and injure the ship."

"No, I think not. To be sure, it is not worth much; yet I do not wish to lose it. But come, never mind the worm; we have seen but one;—put it in."

The stick was accordingly put in. The ship was finished, and as she was launched off into the waters, all ready for the seas, she looked beautiful as the swan when the breeze ruffles his white, feathered bosom, as he sits on the waters. She went to sea, and for a number of years did well. But it was found, on a distant voyage, that she grew weak and rotten. Her timbers were found all eaten away by the worms. But the captain thought he would try to get her home. He had a great, costly load of goods in the ship, such as silks, crapes, and the like, and a great many people. On their way home, a storm gathered. The ship for a while climbed up the high waves, and then plunged down, creaking, and rolling finely. But she then sprang a leak. They had two pumps, and the men worked at them day and night; but the water came in faster than they could pump it out. She filled with water; and she went down under the dark, blue waters of the ocean, with all the goods and all the people on board. Every one perished. Oh, how many wives, and mothers, and children, mourned over husbands, and sons, and fathers, for whose return they were waiting, and who never returned! And all, all this, probably, because that little stick of timber, with the worm in it, was put in, when the ship was built! How much property, and how many lives, may be destroyed by a little worm! And how much evil may a man do, when he does a small wrong, as that man did who put the wormy timber in the ship!

Suppose a little boy were walking out in the fields on some fair day of autumn. As he bounds along, he sees something on the ground, which looks round and smooth, like a little egg. He picks it up. It is an acorn. He carries it a little

90

while, and then throws it away. It is a small affair, and useless. He forgets it entirely. The poor little acorn lies forgotten. The ox comes along, and treads it in the ground without ever knowing it. It lies and sleeps there in the ox-track during the cold winter. In the spring, it swells. The little sprout peeps out; a root grows down, and two little leaves open on the top of the ground. It lives and grows. During a hundred years it grows, while men live and die, and while many a storm beats upon it. It is now a giant oak. It is made into a mighty ship, and laden with goods; she sails round the world, and does her errands at many hundreds of places. She bears the flag of her nation on her mast, and her nation is honored for her sake. What great things may spring from small ones! Who would have thought that such a little thing could contain the mighty oak in it? Besides this, that one tree bears acorns enough, every year; to raise a thousand more oaks; and these, every year, bear enough to rear ten thousand more. Thus a whole forest may be shut up in the little bud of a single acorn. What great things may be found in little things!

I wish to have you see this so clearly, that you cannot forget it, because it will be of great use to you, all the way through life, if remembered.

In a dark night, there was once a ship coming into one of our harbors. She had been to India on a long voyage, and had been gone a year or two. She had a very costly cargo, or load, on board. The captain and all in her were hoping and expecting soon to see their friends, and their homes. The sailors had brought out their best clothes, and were clean and neat. As they came bounding along over the foaming waters, and drew near to the land, the captain told a man to go up to the top of the mast, and "look out for the lighthouse." The lighthouse is a high, round kind of a tower, built out on the points of the land, with great lamps lighted every night in its top, so that vessels may see it before they get too near the land. This lighthouse stood at the entrance of the harbor.

Pretty soon, the man cried out, "Light ahead!" Then they all rejoiced, and knew they were near the harbor.

Now, while they had been gone, this lighthouse had been removed to another place. But the captain knew nothing about that. So they kept sailing in what, they supposed, was the old way. In a short time, the man at the mast-head cries out, "Breakers ahead!" that is, rocks just before us, and the ship is just upon them. The captain just cast his eye out on the dark waters, and saw the white foam of the rocks. In a moment, he cries out, "Starboard the helm."[46] Now, see how much may hang on one little word. The man at the helm mistook the word, and thought the captain said, "Larboard the helm."[47] So he turned it the wrong way. It was done in a moment, in the twinkling of an eye. But it was turned the wrong way; and the ship struck on the rocks the next moment, and was dashed in a thousand pieces. The cargo was lost, and every soul on board, except one or two, were drowned. All this hung upon one little word, one little mistake. If that word had been understood right, she would not have been lost. One single mistake, small as it seemed to be, brought about all this ruin and death. Do you not see how plain it is, that great results may turn upon very small things? One moment of time turned the scale, and property and lives all go down into the deep. There the goods are destroyed, and there the human beings bodies sleep till the great morning of the resurrection-day.

In the new country, that is, in those new states where the great forests are not cut down, and where only a few people live, the fire sometimes, when it is dry in the autumn, gets into the woods. It burns the dry leaves, the dry limbs and twigs, and dry trees, and even the green trees. Sometimes it gets so hot, that nobody can go near it. It leaps from tree to tree, burning and crackling, and rushing on like a fierce

---

[46] Starboard is the right hand side of the ship.
[47] Larboard is the left hand side of the ship.

army in battle. A thousand war-horses could not make more noise; and, in the night, it throws up its flames, and is seen a great way off. Sometimes it goes almost a hundred miles before it can be stopped. Now, see what this has to do with my Lecture.

A little boy was playing one day just at the edge of the woods. His mother was gone; and though he knew it was wrong, yet he went into the house, and brought out some fire. He felt that it was wrong, but thought that nobody would ever know it. He played with the fire awhile, and it did no hurt. At length, the wind blew a spark into the woods, and the dry leaves caught—they blazed—the whole woods were on fire. On the fire went, kindled into a great flame, raging and burning all before it. For whole days, and even weeks, it roared and raged without hurting any body. But one day, when the wind blew hard, it burned on faster and more awfully. And, as it swept through the forest, it passed by a small, new house, which a poor man had just built, almost in the middle of the forest, on some land which he had just bought. The man was gone away. When at a great distance, he saw the fire, and hastened home as fast as possible. But, oh, what a sight! The woods were all burned black. Not a leaf was left. They looked like a funeral. His little house and barn were burned up, and, what was worse, his faithful wife and little child—all were burned up. On the spot where he left them happy in the morning, nothing was left but a pile of smoking ashes.

All this, all this, because that little boy disobeyed his mother, and played with fire! All this from one little spark of fire! How much, how very much, may hang on little things!

Let me give you one example more. Almost twelve hundred years ago, in a distant country, there was a mother with an infant in her arms. She was not a Christian mother. Now, it would seem as if that little infant was of no consequence. Ten thousand such might die, and the world would hardly know it. It would seem, too, as if it was of no great consequence whether or not that child be instructed about God and Jesus Christ, and be taught to serve God. He was not so taught. What was the result? He grew up, became a man, made a new religion, which is called Mohammedanism. He taught people to believe the most foolish and wicked lies, and to practice the most wicked things. He made them believe that he was a prophet of God, and that God would be pleased to have them kill every body on earth who will not believe Mohammedanism. They are a most bloody, cruel, wicked people. Millions of such have lived, and are now living. And what is worse than all, God says that he will cast them all away into hell forever and ever. Read the 19th chapter of Revelation, and see what an awful doom is before them.

Now, all this seemed to turn upon the point, whether that little infant should be taught to be a Christian or not. Had he belonged to a Sabbath School, and been taught as you are taught, I do believe he would never have told such wicked lies, and led away millions of men after him, who will perish forever. Wicked man! he lived only to do mischief, and began a great evil, which has not yet been checked. How thankful ought you to be, who have Christian mothers to watch over you, to pray for you, and to teach you from the Bible! Else you might not only live in vain, but be lost, and be the means of leading others to eternal ruin. How much good or evil may hang on a single child!

Let me, now, my dear children, tell you what this subject ought to teach you. Let me show you what the great truth, that great results may hang on little things, should teach you.

1. Be careful what you say. The tongue is a little member; but it does immense evil. Let a child drop one wicked word, and another may catch it, and remember it, and follow the example, and become a wicked child and a wicked man. Let a child tell one lie, and he may thus begin a course of lying which will ruin him for this life and the next. Says a good man, speaking of his dear child, then in the grave, "When he was about three years old, an aged female, at whose house he was staying for a day, informed me that William had told a falsehood. I was thunder-struck, and almost distracted; for the information seemed to blast my most cherished hopes. This might, I thought, be the commencement of a series of evils forever ruinous to our peace. I am not sure that my agony, on hearing of his death, was much more intense than that which I then endured, from an apprehension of his guilt. Instantly, but without betraying my emotions, I asked him what he had said. He answered, at once, in so artless a manner, as to convince me that my boy was yet innocent. I pursued the inquiry, and, in a few moments, found, to my inexpressible joy, that he was perfectly correct in all he had stated." You see how a good father abhors a single lie. God abhors it much more. And one lie will lead to others; one wicked word to others; one foolish word to others. Remember that God hears every word, and will call you to an account for every word, at the great Day of Judgment.[48]

2. Be careful what company you keep. You may think of God, and think you will serve him; but one half hour spent in wicked company will drive all that is good far from you. You may hear a wicked word which you never heard before. Where did these children ever hear wicked words? Did their parents teach them these words? No. But you learned every one of them in bad company. Where did you learn wicked thoughts? Surely, nowhere but in bad company.[49] One wicked boy may spoil many more. He may spoil their manners, spoil their language, spoil their innocent feelings, spoil their obedience to God and to their parents. See to it, that you are not thus spoiled. When you hear one word from anybody, which you feel that your parents would not say, be sure that is bad company. Flee from it at once.

---

[48] Matthew 12:36,37.
[49] 1 Corinthians 15:33.

3. Be careful to fear God and live for him every day. Every child can easily form habits of sin. They are formed very easily indeed. One day spent without thinking of God, or praying to him, will prepare for another. One Sabbath broken, will fit you to break another. One day spent in sin, will only fit your heart for sin to dwell in. Would you dig away the dam which keeps in the great mill-pond? You need only dig a little place, and let out a little stream, and the whole will rush through after it. There may be multitudes lost forever, whose ruin might be traced back to their conduct on a single day.

4. Be careful what you do. Do you see a thing which you want, but which is not yours? Do not covet it; for you may thus begin those covetous feelings which will keep you out of heaven. Had Judas not coveted the first thing which he did covet, he would never have been so wicked as to sell the blessed Redeemer. Does your eye see something which you want, and does your little hand want to stretch itself out, and take it? Oh, do it not, do it not! This is stealing. And this may lead you on till you are a thief, till you are shut up in the dungeon, and shut up in hell. Remember that you ought not to do any thing, upon which you cannot go and ask the blessing of God in prayer. The eye of the great God is ever upon you; and your eternity may hang upon the conduct of an hour. Remember this, and be afraid to sin. Amen.

LECTURE XI

FRAGMENTS ALL TO BE SAVED

"Gather up the fragments that remain, that nothing be lost" – John 6:12

The goldsmith's shop. The mountains weighed. The stars named. The little gleaners. Christ feeding the multitude. Wrong to waste things. Wrong to waste money. The deep river. Brimstone matches. The expensive drink. Hamilton's duel. Life wasted. The sailor's dream. The ring. The ring lost. Burning mountains. The ring recovered. The dream supposed to be true and real. Limbs lost. The Bible wasted. The mind ruined. Six things seen. The SOUL—the SOUL.

I suppose most of these children have been into the shop of a goldsmith. A goldsmith is a man who works in gold, and makes beads, and rings, and other things, out of gold. If you have ever been in such a shop, did you see the man work at the gold? What fine and beautiful tools he has! what little saws, and files, and drills to bore with! And then he is very careful not to waste any gold. When he files it, or bores it, he is very careful to have a fine, soft brush, with which to sweep up every grain of gold, even the smallest and finest dust. He is very careful not to lose any fragments.

Did you ever read the 40th chapter of Isaiah? How wonderfully is the great God described there! When he spread out the mighty heavens over our heads, "he measured" them, so as not to have them too large or too small. When he made the great waters, he "measured" them, so as not to have a drop too much or too little. When he made the hills and the lofty mountains, he "weighed the mountains in a scale, and the hills in a balance,"[50] so as to have not a grain of sand, or a single atom, too much or too little; not because God has not water enough, and ground enough, but because he would teach us to *waste* nothing. Every fragment must be saved and used.

Go out, on some bright, star-light evening, and look up. What a multitude of stars! How thick they are! If many of them should go out forever, we should not know it. And if new stars were to be added to them, we should not know it. They may seem useless to us. We cannot count them. But God knows every one, and has not made one too many nor one too few. David says, "He telleth the number of the stars; he calleth them all by their names."[51] What a family! All have names, and all

> "Forever singing, as they shine,
> 'The hand that made us is divine!'"[52]

Have these children never been out in the time of harvest, and seen the men reap the wheat and rye? They cut down the waving grain with the greatest care, and then bind it in bundles, and then carefully carry it home on the cart. They try not to lose any, because every kernel will make a little flour. But after all their care, they do lose some. Some heads of wheat do drop out, and some kernels will shell out. God knew this would be so. But he would have nothing lost; and so he has made "the little gleaners," such as the little bird and the squirrel, to follow the harvest, and pick up the fragments, that nothing be lost.

So Jesus Christ teaches us. He preached out in the open fields, for he had no meeting-house; and, if he had, it would not have held half who wanted to hear him

---

[50] Isaiah 40:12.
[51] Psalm 147:4.
[52] Joseph Addision, "Ode" in *The Spectator*, 1712.

preach. A great many thousands followed him; and when he had taught them for a great while, and found that, under the hot sun, they were weary and hungry, he had them sit down on the grass in companies. I suppose this was so that neighbors and friends might sit together, and, also, so that they might be counted. He blessed the bread, which was only five loaves, and the fishes, which were only two little ones; and they all ate enough. One loaf of bread was enough for a thousand people, after Christ had blessed it. After they had done eating, he told the disciples to gather up the fragments, that nothing be lost. So they gathered up the pieces and the crumbs, and had each of them a basket full. Now, Christ could have made bread enough to feed the world.· He does make enough for every mouth every year. And he could make it at any time. But he would have nothing lost. The twelve baskets of fragments would do for the poor, and do for the disciples at another time.

You see what I am teaching you in this Lecture. It is, *that it is wrong to waste anything.*

Give me your thoughts, and follow what I say, and see if it be not so. Shall I have your close attention? Yes. I see, by the looks of every little boy and every little girl, that I shall.

Suppose you know of a narrow river, where the waters are dark, and almost black. They are deep, too—so deep that no one, with the longest pole, can reach the bottom. The stream runs swift, too; so that, if you drop anything into that river, it sinks, and can never be found again. Now, suppose, just on the bank of this river, a little way back, there is a little cottage. It is very small. And in it is a poor widow and five or six little children. The woman is sick and poor, and can neither work nor buy food for her hungry children. She is in great distress. Suppose a man lives not far off, who has money, a great deal of money. He hardly knows what to do with it. So, every night, he comes just before that cottage, where the poor children are crying for food, and there drops a dollar into that river. It sinks, and is lost forever. To-morrow night he will do so again, and so every night, while that wretched family are starving. Now, does he not do wrong? Has he a right thus to drop his money into the river, and let poor children suffer? No, no; he has no right to do it. But suppose, instead of throwing it in the river, he spends it for something which he does not want, and which will do him no good. Is this right? No. It is wasted, even then. Suppose he spends it for something fine and showy, but which is really of no use. Is that right? No. It is still wasted. You see, then, that it is wrong to waste money, when people are starving.

A Bible can be printed and bound, and sent to a poor family, or to a poor child who has none, for fifty cents. Some gentlemen went out, one day, to ask such as choose to give, for money, in order to send the Bible to the heathen, who have none. They went to one house and another, and at last went up to a house to go in, where they were not acquainted. As they stopped on the door-steps, they overheard the gentleman of the house talking to a girl in the kitchen for wasting a new match every time she wanted to light a candle. This, they thought, was real stinginess.

"Let us go," says one; "we shall get nothing here. A man who scolds about a match will never give anything."

"We can but try," said the other.

They went in, and told their errand. The gentleman took out his purse, and gave them more than any one had done, enough to send a hundred Bibles to the heathen. They were astonished at his giving so much. They told him how they had overheard him talking about the match, and did not expect anything from him.

"Oh, this is the very reason," said the gentleman, "why I can give so much to send the Bible. I allow nothing to be wasted, and thus, by saving all, I have money with which to do good."

But people love to spend their money for handsome and fine things, rather than use it to send the Bible to those who have not any Bible. I know they do. But do they do right? Suppose there is a kind of drink that you love very much. It tastes so good, you could drink a whole tumbler full;—hut this drink, though it does not hurt you now, will, in the end, shorten your life one minute for every drop you taste; one minute for every drop; one hour for every teaspoon full; one year for every tumbler full. Would it be right for you to drink this awful drink, though you do love it? No. No. You know it would not be right. You have no right to waste your own life. You may not throw away a year, nor a fragment. All must be gathered up. Nor have you a right to waste money because you love the useless things which it will buy, any more than to waste life by such a miserable drink.

There was once a man by the name of HAMILTON. He was a great man, a friend of Washington, a friend to his country, and a man who was greatly respected and beloved. But in an evil hour he engaged to fight a duel. It was with a man who never missed his aim, and, therefore, Hamilton felt certain that he should be killed. He told no one. But the evening before, he went to the flower shop, and bought a beautiful hunch of flowers for his wife, and for each of his children. These he carried home, and gave them the evening before the duel. They took them with smiles, little thinking that on the morrow their dear father would be brought home to die. He bade them good night; and the next morning, before any of them had risen, he had fought the duel, and was brought home wounded, and was soon to die. I cannot tell you how that family felt. But I can ask you a question here; was it right for this man thus to throw away his life? He had a right to gather the beautiful roses, and carry them home to wither; but he had no right to fight a duel, and lose his life.

When John Newton was a common sailor, and very wicked, he tells us he had this remarkable dream. "The scene presented to my imagination was the harbor of Venice, where we had lately been. I thought it was night, and my watch upon the deck; and that, as I was walking to and fro by myself, a person came to me (I do not remember from whence), and brought me a ring, with an express charge to keep it carefully; assuring me that, while I preserved that ring, I should be happy and successful; but if I lost or parted with it, I must expect nothing but trouble and misery. I accepted the present and the terms willingly, not in the least doubting my own care to preserve it, and highly satisfied to have my happiness in my own keeping. I was engaged in these thoughts, when a second person came to me, and, observing the ring on my finger, took occasion to ask me some questions concerning it. I readily told him its virtues; and his answer expressed a surprise at my weakness, in expecting such effects from a ring. I think he reasoned with me some time upon the impossibility of the thing; and at length he urged me in direct terms to throw it away. At first I was shocked at the proposal; but his insinuations prevailed. I began to reason and doubt, and at last plucked it off my finger, and dropped it over the ship's side into the water, which it had no sooner touched, than I saw, at the same instant, a terrible fire burst out from a range of mountains (a part of the Alps), which appeared at some distance behind the city of Venice. I saw the hills as distinct as if awake, and that they were all in flames. I perceived, too late, my folly; and my tempter, with an air of insult, informed me, that all the mercy God had in reserve for me was comprised in that ring, which I had willfully thrown away. I understood that I must go with him to the burning mountains, and that all the flames I saw were kindled on my account. I trembled, and was in great agony; so that it was surprising I did not then awake; but my dream continued, and when I thought myself on the point of a constrained departure, and stood self-condemned, without plea or hope, suddenly either a third person, or the same who brought me the ring at first (I am not certain which), came to me, and demanded the cause of my grief. I told him the plain case, confessing that I had ruined myself willfully, and deserved no pity. He blamed my rashness, and asked if I should be wiser, supposing I had my ring again? I could hardly answer to this, for I thought it was gone beyond recall. I believe, indeed, I had no time to answer, before I saw this unexpected friend go down under the water, just in the spot where I had dropped it, and soon returned, bringing the ring with him! The moment he came on board, the flames in the mountains ceased, and my seducer left me. Then was 'the prey taken from the hand of the mighty, and the lawful captive delivered.'[53] My fears were at an end, and, with joy and gratitude, I approached my kind deliverer to receive the ring again; but he refused to return it, and spoke to this effect: 'If you should be entrusted with this ring again, you would very soon bring yourself into the same distress. You are not able to keep it, but I will preserve it for you, and whenever it is needful, will produce it in your behalf.' Upon this I awoke in a state of mind not to be described."

This was a dream; but had it been real, and had the ring been a real ring, and able to make him happy as long as he kept it, I ask you, if he would not have done wrong, and have been very wicked, in throwing it away into the sea? I know you will say, "Yes." Had all of these dear children a ring put on their

---

[53] Isaiah 49:20.

first finger, which could make them happy as long as they kept it, would they not be foolish, and wicked, to throw it away? Suppose you had such a ring, and, as you went home, you should meet with a wicked child, who should try to persuade you to throw it away,—would you not do wrong to listen to him a single moment?

Suppose that you are very fond of a certain kind of food. It does not hurt you now, but some time hence it will hurt you. It will cause you to lose a finger, and then an arm, and then a foot. Would it be right for you to eat it, though you were fond of it? You all say, No, it would not be right. Our hands, and our arms, and our feet, are too valuable to be wasted in this manner.

If each of you had a beautiful new Bible given you, and it was the only one you could ever have in this world, would it not be wrong to throw it away? Would it not be wrong to tear out its leaves and burn them? Would it not be wrong to take a pen and blot out whole verses, so that you could not read them? Yes, I am sure you will all say, yes, it would be wrong. And why? Because the Bible is too valuable to be wasted.

Suppose you know of a fine little boy, who behaves well, and learns well, and who has a bright eye, and a bright mind looking out of that eye. He is the hope of his parents. He may make a minister of the gospel, or a very useful man, if he lives. And suppose that two or three of these children should get together and lay a plan to scare that little boy on some dark night. They do it. They scare the poor child so much that he loses his reason, and will be crazy all the rest of his life! I ask you, would not this be very wicked, very wrong? I know you will say, Yes, yes. And why? Because the *mind* is too valuable to be thus wasted and destroyed in sport. Very true.

Now, if you have heard what I have been saying, you see,

1.   That it is wrong to waste *property,* because it is too valuable. Christ would not allow the crumbs to be wasted. Property will feed and clothe the poor, and send the Bible to those who have none.

2.   That it is wrong to waste our *lives,*—because life is too valuable to be thrown away.

3.   That it is wrong to waste our *happiness,*—it is too precious. That it is wrong to waste our *limbs,* such as hands and feet.

4.   That it would be wrong to waste and throw away the *Bible,* or any part of it.

5.   That it would be very wrong to destroy the *mind,* even of a child, because the mind is too valuable to be wasted.

And now, dear children, what shall I say to you of the soul—the soul—which will never die? If it be wrong to waste other things, is it not much more so to throw away your thoughts, your feelings, and, at last, your soul itself? Oh, you may be careful of property, and of life, and happiness, and limbs, and the Bible, and the mind; but if you neglect the soul, and do not see to that, you are miserable forever. All other things are nothing, of no value, when laid by the side of the soul. I beg you, then, as you gather up the fragments about the soul, not to forget and neglect the soul itself. That must live forever. Amen.

LECTURE XII

THE SABBATH TO BE KEPT HOLY

Remember the Sabbath-day, to keep it holy. –Ex. 20.8

Picture-books. Parables of Christ. A new parable. The offer. The wreck of the ship. THE LIFE-BOAT. The life-boat in use. The parable explained. The foolish excuses. Who would be a thief? The poor beggar. The house broken open. Little thieves. What makes people poor. A strong reason. STORY by the Author. Duty put off. The school not together. The foolish superstition. What makes a man stupid? The corpse. Mill going on the Sabbath. Little boy crushed by the wheel. Sad thoughts. Scene remembered. Instruction. Poetry. Conclusion.

Children your little books are full of pictures. One has in it the picture of a horse; another has a house, trees, rivers, birds, and hills. Suppose I wanted to make a little boy understand about a lion, how he looks, how he acts, and the like. What would be the best way? The best way would be to lead him out, and let him see a lion. But if I could not do it, the next best way would be to show him the *picture* of a lion. This picture would give him a better idea of it than anything I could tell him about a lion.

Just so Jesus Christ used to preach. He used to teach in parables, which are a kind of picture-preaching. In this way, he used to make things plain and very interesting to those who heard him. Now, I am going to give you a parable. Try and see if you can understand it, and remember it.

There was once a good man who was very rich. I cannot stop to tell you all the good things which he did, but will mention only one. He built a large and beautiful ship all at his own expense. He fitted up the ship with a

Pilot who knew the coast, and a helm by which to steer her, and a compass to point out the way they were sailing. She had everything ready. He then called his friends together, and said, "See, here is a beautiful ship, filled with costly goods, and all fitted and ready to sail. Everything is ready. You may have her, and have everything on board. You may go and trade where you please, on *one* condition. Not one of you may carry or drink a drop of ardent spirit.[54] This is the only condition I make; and I make this, because, otherwise, you will get the ship on the rocks, and will all be lost." The men take the ship on this condition, and set sail for a distant country. They had been out on the water but a little while, before one of them brought forward some ardent spirit, which he said he had taken for sickness, and to make him feel better, though he had no wish to disobey him who gave them the ship. So he drank; and, one by one, they all drank, till they knew not how to manage the ship. They were intoxicated by the drink. Then came on the dark night. The cold, wet winds blew, and the whole ocean foamed and rolled up its great waves most fearfully. The ship was carried onward and onward, till she struck upon a great flat rock. Here she turned on one side, and lay, every moment creaking, as if going to pieces. The people on board were too much intoxicated to do anything. The morning comes, and it is cold, and the spray of the water, upon the poor ship, freezes in a moment, and the people are chilled, and cold, and hardly able to hold themselves where they are. They have gotten over their intoxication just enough to know where they are. The shore is near, but no one can get to it. The high waves roll and dash, and a boat cannot go from the shore to the ship. It would be turned over and sunk in a moment. The people all gather down on the shore, and see the ship, and the freezing people on board, but cannot help them.

---

[54] *Ardent spirit* is a euphemistic term for strong alcoholic beverage.

But, look! who is that man who hastens down to the water's side? It is the good man who fitted up the ship, and gave her to these people. He sees they have disobeyed him, and ruined the ship, but he feels deeply for them. What is he going to do? See there! He has built a little boat of costly materials, and made it to hold air, and filled it with his own breath. That little boat cannot be sunk. It will live and swim anywhere. It is called the LIFE-BOAT, because it can go out on the stormy water, and save the lives of perishing men who are shipwrecked. It is now launched out on the waters! But who is in it? It is the only son of that good man! See! it bounds and drives from wave to wave like a feather—straight to the ship! The poor people on board gaze upon it. They are perishing! There, now, one has dropped over in the waves, and is lost! No,—the life-boat has picked him up! One and another gets in, and the little boat shoots, off over the stormy water for the shore. Again and again it comes, and will hasten backwards and forwards all day, till dark, so that *all* may have the opportunity of getting on shore, if they please. But some are ashamed to see the face of that good man on shore, and so they hesitate, and do not get into the life-boat. They had rather perish where they are.

Now, tell me, is not that a very kind and good man? You all say, "Yes." And is not that life-boat an admirable contrivance? You all say, "Yes." And are not those who will not get into it very foolish? "Yes. Indeed."

Well, then, you have my parable. Do you understand it? The world is the ship, and God is the good man who built it, and gave it to us. We have become intoxicated with sin, are ruined, and lost. The SABBATH is the life-boat, which comes regularly from the shores of eternity, and offers to carry us near to God, and to safety.

But I want to talk a little longer about this shipwreck, and this life-boat; and I do it so that you need not forget it. He who neglects or refuses to keep the Sabbath holy, refuses to leave the wreck of the ship, and chooses to brave the storms and the ruin which will one day consume the whole world to ashes. Is this wise? Is this safe? Is this being grateful to God? Suppose some one on the wreck of the ship should laugh at the little life-boat, and say, "It can never carry any one to the shore." Would it be wise to mind him? Suppose some should say, "We are too busy, and we wish to drink a little more of that intoxicating drink, before we go." Would that be wise, and should others do like them? Suppose others, again, should say, "We intend to go in the boat before night, but as we are ashamed to see the face of the good man whom we have disobeyed, we will not go now, but will wait awhile." Is this wise? Is this safe?

Just so people do, who neglect to keep the Sabbath holy. They hear others speak lightly of religion, and so they let this life-boat come and go, once every week, and do not improve it. Or they are busy, and want to drink in more sin, and so they say, "Not now." Or they are ashamed to go and confess to God, and so they say they are going to improve the Sabbath, and serve God at some future time, before the night of death comes; but are not yet ready. Is this wise? Will you be like them? I trust not.

Who would be a thief? I suppose there is not a child present who does not think it very mean, and low, and wicked, to steal. You would despise the little boy who would put your ball or your top into his pocket, and thus steal it; and the little girl who would put a doll or a pin-cushion in her bag, and carry it home, would be despised as mean and wicked. But suppose a poor man, who was without any home, should come to your house, almost without clothing, and very hungry. You all at once pity him. You give him food to eat, and your mother looks him up some clothing. And as he goes away, warm and comfortable, your father says to him, "Here, poor man, here are *six* dollars. I have but *seven* in the world, and give you six of them, and will keep only the seventh for myself and family." Would not this be very kind and generous of your father? I know you all think it would. But suppose that poor man went away, not thankful in the least, and, in the night, came back, and broke into your house, and stole that *seventh* and *last* dollar which your father has. What would he deserve? Why, he would almost deserve the gallows. He would be an ungrateful monster, and a vile thief. But suppose, also, that, in breaking into the house, to get the dollar, he had to kill several members of the family. What now do you say? Is any punishment too severe? But take care, or you pass sentence upon yourself.

We are the poor man, and God has but seven days in the week. He gives us six of these, in which to "labor and do all our work,"[55] and keeps only the seventh for himself. And the man, or the woman, or the child, who breaks the Sabbath, steals from God. Yes, he robs God. And, in doing it, he sets a wicked example, which kills the

---

[55] Exodus 20:9.

souls of others. Is not this stealing? Will you remember, then, that when you break the Sabbath, you steal from God? Are there no little thieves present, who have often thus stolen from God? Now, will God bless you and prosper you in doing so?

You see why the families who break the Sabbath, and who do not go to meeting, are generally so poor and so miserable. It is because they steal from God every seventh day of their lives; and God will not, and does not bless them in it. Merchants who keep their counting-rooms open on the Sabbath, generally fail in business, and lose all the property they have. A gentleman took notice, in New York, for twenty-five years, that every merchant who thus broke the Sabbath, failed, without a single exception. And a great lawyer in this country, who helped to try very many for murder, says, that they all began their wickedness by breaking the Sabbath.

I have a strong reason why I feel very anxious to have these children remember the Sabbath day, and keep it holy. And I will now give you this strong reason.

Many years ago, while I was in college, I opened a Sabbath School in a distant, neglected neighborhood, yet within the limits of the town. At first, the project was greatly ridiculed, and many opposed. But ridicule and opposition soon give way to a good cause, and in a short time I had seventy students. The room in which we met was an unfinished chamber of a poor, lame woman—the only place that was offered. The floor was not nailed down, and neither ceiling nor plaster had ever been seen in the chamber. The chimney passed up in the centre, and the bare rafters were over our heads. Yet never did I see brighter or happier faces than among the little groups with which I regularly met. They lived so far from meeting, that few could attend; or, rather, their parents felt too indifferent to carry them; so that their Sabbath School embraced all that was Sabbath to them. It is now many years since, and I suppose they have all grown up, or have been removed into eternity by this time; but I can never forget this, my first Sabbath School, nor the happy countenances which composed it.

One hot Sabbath, I had walked out to meet my Sabbath School, and, at the close of the lessons, I felt weary and unwell. The children were expecting me to give them a history of the holy Sabbath, from its first appointment, and to tell them *why* God appointed it, and what are our *duties* in regard to it; for so I had promised them, and had in fact prepared myself to do it. But, being weary and unwell, I told them that, for these reasons, I would defer it till the next Sabbath. While thus putting it off, I noticed a bright little boy, sitting near me, who seemed to look disappointed. He had expected to hear about the holy Sabbath. Oh, had I remembered how Christ taught the poor woman of Samaria, though he was weary and faint, should I not have done differently?[56]

The next Sabbath came, and my school were again coming together. On arriving at the house, instead of finding them all quiet in their seats, as usual, I found them grouped around the door, some sobbing, others looking frightened—all silent.

On inquiry, they told me that "little Lewis had just been killed by the mill!" This was all they knew about it. At the head of my little flock, I hastened to the house where the little boy lived. At the door I was met by the father of the child, wringing his hands, his face red and swollen, his eyes sunken and glaring, and his breath loaded with the fumes of ardent spirits.

"Oh," cried the man, "I might have known it. I might have known it all!"

"Might have known what, sir?"

"Oh, I might have known that today one of my family must go; but I did not think, could not think, it must be my youngest boy!"

---

[56] See this incident recorded in John 4.

"Pray, how might you have known that one must die today?"

"Why, when I came home last evening, old Rover" (pointing to a stupid old dog that lay crouched under the table) "sat on the door-steps, with his face to the east, howling, and howling. I knew then some one—or I might have known that some one—must go today, but did not think it must be poor little Lewis!"

"Do you believe there is a God?"

"Oh, yes, have no doubt of it."

"And do you suppose he reveals events to a dog, a creature without a soul, and without reason, which he does not reveal to the wisest of men? Nothing is more common than for a dog to howl when his master is gone, and he feels lonely; and as to his face being towards the east, I see nothing strange in that, since your house faces the east."

"Ah, you may say so; but I might have known it would come,"—and again he turned away to sob, and I fear to drink, and then wonder over his being more stupid than his dog.

I led my students into the room. They seemed to breathe only from the top of their lungs. I lifted up the white napkin, and there was little Lewis—a mangled corpse! The children were all hushed as we gazed. The little girls covered their faces with their handkerchiefs and aprons. The little boys wiped their eyes with their hands and with the sleeves of their jackets.

For some weeks, it had been very dry, and the streams had become low. But during the preceding day and night, a heavy rain had fallen. A mill, on a small stream near by, which had stood still for some time for want of water, was set a-going early on Sabbath morning. I need not ask if the miller feared God.

About an hour before the Sabbath School usually came together, little Lewis went down to the mill-stream to swim. The poor boy had never seen his parents keep the Sabbath holy. He swam out into the stream. The current was strong—too strong for him—he raised the cry of distress—the miller heard him and saw him, but was too much frightened to do anything. The current swept along—the little boy struggled—again cried for help—the waters rushed on—he was sucked down under the gate— the great mill-wheel rolled round—crash!—he was in a moment crushed and dead! Scarcely had his last cry reached the ears of the miller, before his mangled corpse came out from under the wheel. *It was the same little boy who had looked so disappointed on the last Sabbath, because I omitted to talk about the holy Sabbath.*

While standing beside the lifeless clay of this fair child, with all the children about me, my feelings were awful indeed. It seemed as if every child would cry out, "Oh, had you kept your word, and told us about breaking the Sabbath, he would not have gone into the water—he would not have lain there dead." It seemed as if the lips, though sealed by the hand of death, would open and reproach me. "Had I not put off my duty, probably this life would have been saved—perhaps an undying soul would have been saved from the guilt of being the everlasting enemy of God. What sacrifices would I not make, could that child once more come into my Sabbath School?" Such were my thoughts. I have never been able to look back upon that scene without keen anguish. I have sometimes mentioned it to Sabbath School teachers, and, by it, urged them never to put off till the next Sabbath any duty which can be performed on this. And since I have been a minister, when I have felt weary and feeble, and tempted to put off some duty to a more convenient season, I have recalled that scene to my mind; and truly thankful shall I feel in the great judgment day, if you, my dear children, will learn from this simple story two things.

Lecture Twelve: *The Sabbath Kept Holy*

1. *To remember and keep holy the Sabbath day.* Had that dear child only obeyed this one short text, he would not have been called to the presence of God while in the very act of sin.

> "This day belongs to God alone;
> He makes the Sabbath for his own;
> And we must neither work nor play
> Upon God's holy Sabbath day.
>
> 'Tis well to have one day in seven,
> That we may learn the way to heaven;
> Or else we never should have thought
> About his worship as we ought.
>
> And every Sabbath should be passed
> As if we knew it were our last;
> For what would dying people give
> To have one Sabbath more to live!"

2. *Never to put off any duty, or any opportunity to do good, because you do not feel like doing it now.* You may never have the opportunity again.

Should you live and grow up, I have no doubt but you will be prospered and happy, that you will be respected and useful, very much as you keep the Sabbath. God will honor those who honor him.[57] He does not ask us even to open the doors of his house for nothing; no, he will repay us in this life, and in the life to come, with everlasting blessings. May all these great rewards be yours, my dear children, by your keeping his commandments. Amen.

---

[57] 1 Samuel 2:30.

LECTURE XIII

THE GRAVE LOSING ITS VICTORY

O grave, where is thy victory? –1 Cor.15:55

Vapor of morning. Garden-flowers. What is a *buoy?* The drowning man clinging to the buoy. Morning after the storm. Who must die. The twins. Beautiful poetry. Who can die happy? My sister's grave--and the two little boys. Reflections in a grave-yard. The soul lives after the body dies. The humming-bird. The island. The adventurer—his return—his tidings—his death. Meaning of the story. The Christian's death. Angel's conversation. Beautiful description of heaven. Conclusion of the Lectures.

The Bible, my dear children, talks a great deal about the shortness of our lives. Did you ever get up in some October morning, and see a thick vapor or fog hanging over the wide meadows and fields? You could not see a man, or even a great tree, at a little distance, the fog was so thick. But go out a few hours afterwards, when the sun is up, and where is all this vapor gone? It is all melted away, and has left no mark on anything. Such, the Bible says, is the life of man. You may look upon a great congregation today, and see the street full of people, and in a few short years they are all gone —and forgotten, like the vapor.

Did you ever walk along the street, and stop and look into a garden, and admire the beautiful flowers which were waving in rows each side of the alley? I presume you have. What colors! How many kinds! See that tulip—that pink—that rose! How beautiful! But wait a few short months, and then stop there again. Where *now* are those flowers? All faded and gone; all dead and passed away. Just so, says the Bible, do we all, even the fairest among men, die and pass away as the flower.[58]

---

[58] Isaiah 40:6; 1 Peter 1:24.

116

Now, why do men all die? Do they wish to die? No, far from it. Let any man be sick, and be in danger of dying, and what will he not do, rather than die? Why, he will swallow as much bitter, disgusting medicine as the doctor wishes him to. He will let him cut off his arm or his leg, or cut out his eye,—or do anything, if he may only live. Men had rather do anything than die. For the most part, they are unwilling even to think of death, and contrive to think of ten thousand things rather than that.

Do you know what a *buoy* is? I will tell you. When a river runs into the sea, the bed in which it runs, along is called the channel; and at the place where it goes into the sea, the water is deeper in the channel than anywhere else; so that, when vessels would go up a river from the great sea, they try to keep in the channel, so as to be in deep water. But how shall they know where the channel is? In this *way*. The people who know where the channel is, take a great stone, and tie a rope to it, and let it sink just in the middle of the channel. At the other end of the rope is a large, round, pine stick, or log, tied. This log floats upon the water, and is held in its place by the stone at the bottom. Well, this log is called a *buoy*, and the sailors steer just alongside of the buoys, when they would go safe.

During an awfully stormy day, a vessel was seen coming towards the shore. The men could not manage her. The people on shore saw her, but could do nothing. There were some great rocks out from the shore, a mile or two; and onward she drove towards those rocks. Soon she was upon them—dash—and was split all in pieces. The people on shore could see it all, but had no life-boat, or any means by which to help them. Were the poor sailors all drowned? No,—there was one poor fellow who floated awhile. They watch him. All the rest are gone. Now he tries to swim a little. There! he has caught hold of a *buoy*, and clings to it for life. O, if they could only get to him!

but they cannot. There he hangs, and rises and falls on each wave—still clinging to the buoy. Is he willing to die? No, he would hang there years, if he could, rather than to die. And now it is night; the sun goes down; the darkness begins to come over the dark waters; and the people sigh, and begin to go home, leaving the poor sailor still holding on to the buoy for his life. One by one they go away, and then turn, and turn round again, to see if they can see him. The last man now goes: it is dark, and he turns and looks. Can he see the buoy and the man? No!—yes, yes, he is still there! They go to their homes; they pray for that poor sailor; they dream about him; they think much of him. The morning comes. The sun rises fair, and the people had hastened down as soon as the light broke in the east, to see if the poor man was there. The storm had gone past, and the buoy was still floating there. But where was the sailor? All, he was gone, gone to the bottom, and will be seen no more till the resurrection day. is it not plain, that we know that every body dreads to die? Why, then, must every body die? The Bible tells us, "Death hath passed upon all men, in that all have sinned."[59] Yes, all are sinners, and must therefore die. The old, gray-headed man must soon go. Death will not respect his silver locks. He will put him in the grave. The man in middle-life is cut down, too, though wife and children may weep and pray against it. The fair youth and the sweet child are not spared; and I think I have never had my heart more affected, than when called to attend the funeral of children. I have seen them in the coffin, when they looked so fair and beautiful, that it seemed hard to bury them up in the ground. The beautiful lines which I am now about to read you, very accurately describe what ministers must often see. They describe two

---

[59] Romans 5:12.

little twin babes, dead, and in the coffin, and the mother bending over it, and looking upon them through her tears.

"'Twas summer, and a Sabbath eve,
And balmy was the air:
I saw a sight which made me grieve—
And yet the sight was fair
Within a little coffin lay
Two lifeless babes, as sweet as May.

Like waxen dolls, which infants dress,
Their little bodies were;
A look of placid happiness
Did on each face appear.
And in the coffin, short and wide, .
They lay together, side by side.

A rose-bud, nearly closed, I found
Each little hand within,
And many a pink was strewed around,
With sprigs of jessamine;
And yet the flowers that round them lay
Were not to me more fair than they.

Their mother, as a lily pale,
Sat by them on a bed,
And, bending o'er them, told her tale,
And many a tear she shed;
Yet oft she cried, amidst her pain,
'My babes and I shall meet again!'"

Do you know what it was that gave comfort to this weeping mother, as she saw her dear twin babes in the coffin? It was the hope of the gospel;—hope, that Jesus Christ would watch over them in the grave, and at last raise them from the long sleep of death, and that she would be allowed to meet them again in heaven, to part from them no more. Yes, the gospel of Christ gives us that blessed hope. "I heard a voice from heaven saying, 'Write, Blessed are the dead who die in the Lord; yea,' saith the Spirit, 'from henceforth, for they rest from their labors, and their works do follow them.'"[60] For this reason, we cannot go and stand by the grave of a Christian, without having hope spring up in the breast. It may be the grave of some dear friend; but if he died a Christian, we feel that Christ will one day come to that grave, and awake his sleeping disciple.

A short time ago, just at sunset, on a summer's day, I went to the grave of a dear sister of mine. Her two little boys went with me. When we had arrived there, I saw four little rose-bushes standing, two at the head and two at the foot of the grave, bending over, as if to meet and hang over the grave.

"That is her grave—our mother's grave," said one of the boys.

"And those rose-bushes"—said I, as the tears started in my eyes,

"Those," said the eldest, "brother and I, and father, set out soon after she was laid there. Those two at the head she planted in the garden herself, and we took them up, and set them there, and call them "mother's bushes.""

"And what do you remember about your dear mother, my boys?"

"Oh, everything."

"What, in particular?"

"Oh, this, uncle, that there never was a day since I can remember, in which she did not take us to her closet, and pray with us, unless she was sick on the bed!"

Never did that sister seem so dear to me as at that moment; and never did my heart feel so full a hope in the words which were engraved on the tomb-stone:

---

[60] Revelation 14:13.

"No mortal woes
Can reach the peaceful sleeper here,
While angels watch her soft repose."

Dear·children, you and I must die, because we are sinners. And every grave that is dug and filled up, is a new monument to show that men are all sinners. Men sometimes are so foolish as to deny that there ever was a flood, which drowned all the world in a few days; but they cannot deny that death now sweeps off the whole world once in about thirty years. Go to that grave-yard yonder. How full of graves! You tread on some sleeper at every step. "Who slew all these?" Suppose you should go to a great prison, full of little cells, and every cell had a prisoner chained in it, and the number was as great as the number of graves in that grave-yard. Would you not think to yourself, "Here must be a great deal of guilt and sin, in order to fill all these cells?" And the grave-yard is the prison-house where God has confined so many prisoners. There is no grave in heaven, and there never would have been one on earth, had it not been for sin.

What a beautiful piece of workmanship is destroyed when one of these children die! The hands hang motionless; the bright eye is closed and dull in darkness; the fresh cheek is pale and cold; the tongue is silent; and the whole body, like a broken vessel, is in ruins. But we may rejoice that the disciple of Christ may go shouting into the grave, "O grave, where is thy victory?" Christ himself has been in it, and sanctified it, and blessed it. Besides, the grave can only receive and claim the poorer part of us. It only takes the body; while the soul, the immortal part, escapes its power. You know you can seem to see things when the eye is shut, and you dream of things when asleep. And so the soul can live, and think, and act, when the body is in the grave. You will sleep in the grave a long, long time, but not always. God can, and will raise up the body again. He is able. Do you see that beautiful little humming-bird dancing from flower to flower, like a spirit of flowers? He was once confined to the little mummy shell; but God brought him out. See that looking-glass: how perfectly you can see your face and form, and every hair on your forehead in it! But had you seen the coarse sand lie on the seashore, before the workmen began, would you think that they could make such a thing from that sand? So God will raise us up from the grave by his wisdom and power.

Oh, how much do we owe to Jesus Christ! At the opening of every grave I seem to hear the angel say, "Come, see the place where the Lord lay."[61] Let me show you what Christ has done here for us.

Suppose we lived upon a great island, entirely surrounded by the great waters. As we looked, we could see nothing but the waters and the sky. We had no ships with which to go away; and there we all lived. We had farms, and shops, and stores, and things just as we now have, with no difference, except we were on an island. One thing more. Every few days, there came a great ship to our island, and the men landed and caught our neighbors and friends, and carried them to the ship, and sailed away, out of sight; in a few days, another ship, and another; and so continually they came, and carried off old and young, friends and neighbors, and we knew nothing what became of them. We wept, and mourned, and feared for ourselves, but we knew not what to do. At length, we see a man rush suddenly down to the shore with a little vessel, which he has built himself at his own expense. He jumps into it alone, and spreads his little sails, and goes off on the great ocean, following those awful ships, to see what has become of our friends. We watch the poor, frail

---

[61] Matthew 28:6.

boat till it is out of sight, wondering if he will ever come to us again. In the mean time, the dark, dreadful ships continue to come and catch away our friends. We look out, and wonder what has become of our dear friend in his boat; for he told us, that, if he found our friends who had been carried off, he would come back to us, with a white flag at the top of his mast. At length, the boat comes in sight! Yes, there she comes, and the white flag streaming at mast-head! Yes, he has found our friends! The crowds all rush down to the water-edge to hear his tidings. The little vessel comes to the shore, and our friend leaps out on the land. We cry out, "What news? What tidings of our friends? Have you found them?"

"Yes, I have found them."
"Are they alive?"
"Yes, all alive."
"Are they happy? What are they doing?"

123

"Oh, they are all carried to a distant country, by the king's ships. When they get there, they are put to a kind of trial, and those who can bear that trial well, are made honorable, and happy, and have most delightful homes, and would not come back here for a world. While those who cannot bear the trial, are sent away to the deserts, and are wretched."

"But will the ships come any more?"

"Yes, they will come again, and again, and carry you all off. But you may all fit yourselves for the trial; and then you will be very happy, and need not fear to go."

"But what? How can we fit ourselves? What shall we do? Oh, tell us quickly, for the ships may be here before we are ready."

"I cannot tell you now. I am dying with fatigue. Here, do you see this book which I take out of my bosom? This tells you all what and how to do. It is plain, and full of instruction. Obey it, and you will all be happy. See, because I could do no other way, I opened my own veins, and have written it with my own blood, and the blood came directly from my heart before I had finished it. Oh, take it, as the last and best pledge of my love."

He ceases to speak, and, worn out with fatigue, he drops down dead on the spot! Oh, what a friend!—and what a book that must be!

You understand me, do you not? We are on that island; and diseases are the dreadful ships which come and carry us off; and eternity is that distant world where we are carried; and Christ is that dear friend who went through the grave into eternity; and the Bible is the book which he has written for us, to prepare us for our trial at the great judgment; and he poured out his soul unto death in thus preparing us to go into eternity and live in happiness. What a friend do those reject and despise, who do not love Jesus

Christ! What a book do those neglect, who live from day to day without reading or thinking about the Bible!

All will come up from the grave at once, but not all to share alike. Just so the chief butler and the chief baker were both let out of the prison at the same time, the one to be honored, and the other to be hanged.[62] "Marvel not at this; for the hour is coming in which all that are in their graves shall hear his voice, and shall come forth; they that have done good, unto the resurrection of life; and they that have done evil, unto the resurrection of damnation."[63] The grave has been called the dressing-chamber, in which good people put on their beautiful garments, in which to arise and meet the Lord in the air. But to the wicked and the unholy, it is the prisoner's cell, in which he is shut up, till led forth to execution.

When Christians die, the angels of God come and lead them up to glory, while the body rests and is purified in the grave.[64] "There," say they, "is Mount Zion, the heavenly Jerusalem, the innumerable company of angels, and the spirits of just men made perfect. You are going now," say they, "to the Paradise of God, wherein you shall see the Tree of Life, and eat of the never-fading fruits thereof; and when you come there, you shall have white robes given you, and your walk and talk shall be every day with the King, even all the days of eternity. There shall you not see again such things as you saw when you were in the lower region upon the earth, to wit, sorrow, sickness, affliction, and death, 'for the former things have passed away.' You are going now to Abraham, to Isaac, to Jacob, and to the prophets, men that God hath taken away from

---

[62] Genesis 40:1-23 contains this entire account. Read it for yourself.

[63] John 5:28.

[64] The following section is taken from John Bunyan's immortal classic called *Pilgrim's Progress*. This is the account of heaven given to Christian as he was standing on the Enchanted Ground.

the evil to come, and that are now 'resting upon their beds, each one walking in his righteousness.'

"What must we do in the holy place?"

"You must there receive the comforts of all your toil, and have joy for all your sorrow; you must reap what you have sown, even the fruit of all your prayers, and tears, and sufferings for the King, by the way. In that place, you must wear crowns of gold, and enjoy the perpetual sight and vision of the Holy One; for there 'you shall see him as he is.'[65] There, also, you must serve him continually with praise, with shouting, and thanksgiving, whom you desired to serve in the world, though with much difficulty, because of the infirmity of your flesh. There your eyes shall be delighted with seeing, and your ears with hearing the pleasant voice of the Almighty One. There you shall enjoy your friends again, that are gone thither before you; and there you shall with joy receive even every one that follows into the holy places after you. There, also, you shall be clothed with glory and majesty, and put into an equipage fit to ride out with the King of Glory. When he shall come with sound of trumpet in the clouds, as upon the wings of the wind, you shall come with him; and when he shall sit upon the throne of judgment, you shall sit by him: yea, and when he shall pass sentence upon all the workers of iniquity, let them be angels or men, you shall also have a voice in that judgment, because they were his and your enemies. And when he shall again return to the city, you shall go too, with sound of trumpet, and be ever with him."

Such, my dear children, will be the glory of every one who obeys God and loves the Redeemer; and such your glory, when you come up from the grave, if you obey God. I must now take my leave of you. Many of you, who read these lines, I shall never know, and never see, till the great Day of Judgment. Oh, if one of you shall be made wise

---

[65] 1 John 3:2.

unto eternal life by this Lecture, I shall have more joy when we meet, than if I had been able to give you a kingdom. Do not put off religion till you are old. You may die within a week. Seek the Savior while he may be found. Call upon him while he is near.[66] Read his word. Obey his voice. Commit yourself, each of you, to his hands. Then the grave will only be a place to sleep in, while God prepares for you a house not made with hands, an everlasting mansion of glory—eternal in the heavens. Amen.

---

[66] Isaiah 55:6,7.

LECTURE XIV

HEAVEN

"In the beginning God created the heaven." – Genesis 1:1

Shape of the earth. Inside of the world. High chimneys. Creating and forming things. Light made first. The three heavens. First heaven. Second and third heaven. Beautiful things. What a throne will be. Society of heaven. How they look in heaven. Why the beautiful things of earth not to be saved. Our friends. Heaven a place.

You know, children, that the earth is round, like an orange. If you were to make a hole through an orange, and then measure the length of that hole, you would find it took three times that length to reach round the orange. And were a hole dug straight through the earth, it would take three times the length of that hole to reach round the earth. Suppose such a hole dug through the earth, and you could walk through it, going a mile every day, how long do you think it would take you to get through? It would take you eight thousand days, which is almost twenty-two years. And it would take you over sixty years to walk round the world, going at the same rate. What a great world! And what do you suppose we should find away down in the earth? I suppose rocks and stones, and some great rivers, and a great deal of fire! A great deal of fire, say you? Yes, a great deal of fire, and it is the heaving of this fire which makes earthquakes, and it is this which makes volcanoes. Volcanoes are always in the tops of very high mountains, which seem to be a kind of chimney, through which these great fires send out their belchings and flames. One of these openings which I call chimneys, on the top of a high mountain on the Sandwich Islands, is ten miles across. What a chimney, to be ten miles across its top! And a few years ago it sent out a river of fire which ran down the mountain two miles wide and forty miles long before it reached the sea, when it plunged into the great ocean. What fires, then, must there be inside of the earth! And how easy for God to make these fires burn up the world at the last day, as he has said in 2 Peter 3. 10: "But the day of the Lord will come as a thief in the night; in the which the heavens shall pass away with a great noise, and the elements shall melt with fervent heat; the earth also, and the works that are therein, shall be burned up."

Men can form things, but they cannot create. They can dig up some ore and make it into the wheels of the watch, or into the little springs which keep the watch going. They can take some coarse, heavy sand, into which you cannot look and see a pin, if it were buried ever so little way, and they can melt this sand and make it into the pure clear glass which you see in these windows, and through which you can see almost as well as if there was no glass there. Men can dig up the different kinds of earth and burn them, and make them into the beautiful colors with which they paint the faces of men, the trees, the waters, or anything they please. But, though we can change and fashion things, and make them curious and useful, we cannot create anything out of nothing. But this is what God did when he created worlds. He formed them out of nothing. He made the light, but he had no sun or anything else to help him do it. He created the world and the heavens, but he made them out of nothing. *How could he* do it? *He* said, "Let there be light, and there was light."[67] "He spake, and it was done; He commanded. and it stood fast."[68]

---

[67] Genesis 1:3.
[68] Psalm 33:9.

I am now going to talk about that part of God's works which are called the heavens. "In the beginning God created the heaven."

Do you recollect that the Bible speaks of three heavens? In Daniel we are told that the angel came from God or the third heaven.[69] And Paul tells us that he was once caught up to the third heaven.[70] Can I make you understand what it means when the Bible speaks of three heavens? Let me try. You know the birds can fly in the air, and the clouds sail in it, and the rain, the dews, and the snows come down out of it. Well, this air is called the heavens. Thus we read of the dews of heaven, the rains of heaven, the clouds of heaven, and the storms of heaven. This is the first heaven. Then above this, far above all this, is the region where the sun and the moon and the stars are. This is the second heaven. "The heavens declare the glory of God, and the firmament showeth his handiwork."[71] And then beyond all this is the place where God and the angels live; and that is what is meant by the third heaven, or, as it is sometimes called, the heaven of heavens.[72]

Thus the first heaven is close to us. We breathe its air. Our birds sing while in it, and our clouds drop the rain out of it. The second heaven contains the sun, moon, and stars, and worlds which we see with the glass which we call the telescope; but we cannot get to it or visit it. The third is what our eye cannot see. It is the place to which Enoch, who walked with God, was taken;[73] where Elijah was carried in the chariot of fire;[74] where Christ is gone and where the saints who arose at his resurrection have gone.[75]

---

[69] Daniel 9:21.
[70] 2 Corinthians 12:2.
[71] Psalm 19:1.
[72] Psalm 148:4; 1 Kings 8:27.
[73] Genesis 5:22-24.
[74] 2 Kings 2:12.
[75] Matthew 27:52.

How wonderful it is that the sun and moon and stars should all be moving and shining, and yet never meet or jar! And sometimes the fiery comet comes blazing up through the sky, with his long trail of light; but God guides him on his way, and he never runs against any other world. What a wonder it is to look out on a bright evening, and see all the stars shining out in their glory, so many worlds! No wonder David says, "When I consider thy heavens, the work of thy fingers, the moon and the stars which thou hast ordained, what is man that thou art mindful of him, and the son of man that thou visitest him?"[76] But what shall I say of the third heaven, where God resides? Who can describe it? Who can tell how it looks? You know what I mean when I compare one thing with another. A tree may look very high, but if you were on the top of a high mountain and were to compare that tree to the mountain, it would look like a small bush. You might call a man handsome, but if you were to compare him with the angels who, John says, were in the tomb of Christ,[77] you would not think him handsome. So we judge of heaven by comparison. We compare it with this world. What would you say should you see God creating a mantle most beautiful and large enough to cover all the earth? He has created such a mantle. It is called *light*.

You have seen the dewdrops hang on the grass and the flowers, like diamonds in the morning sun, have you not? You have seen the sweet flowers all painted by the hand of God, and hung in clusters on the trees. You have seen the gold and purple with which he tinges the morning and the evening sky, now turning the clouds into silver and gold. And how brightly and beautifully do the stars look down upon us as they hang over our heads! What beautiful creatures fly in the air, and swim in the

---

[76] Psalm 8:3,4.
[77] John 20:12.

sea, and what gorgeous shells be on the bottom of the ocean! But this is only the footstool of God, as he calls it. And so we can have an idea of what heaven must be, by comparing a footstool with a throne. What a light must that be which comes not from the sun, nor from the moon, nor from the candle, but directly from the Father of lights? If in this world there are so many beautiful things, what will it be there?

> "If so much loveliness is sent
> To grace our earthly home,
> How beautiful! how beautiful
> Will be the world to come!"

You remember, too, that Peter tells us that this world is to be burned up, to he destroyed. It is not designed to be anything more than a kind of bridge over which men walk from time into eternity; and when it has served its purpose, the old bridge will be taken down. But heaven is never to change. It is never to be burned up, and so God has made it beautiful and glorious. It is the home of all his great family,—the family mansion, —and will it not be beautiful? We know that the tree of life is there, and we know that the river of life, proceeding out of the throne of God and the Lamb, is there.[78] The place is called the Paradise of God, because that garden on earth was so beautiful. But one thing which makes heaven so delightful a place is the people who live there. The angels have their home there. Enoch is there. Moses is there, and his face shines brighter than when he came down from the mountain.[79] Job is there, and his riches will never again be taken from him, for he has in heaven a better and an enduring substance. David is there, with a harp that makes new melody and new sweetness for ever.

[78] Revelation 22:1,2.
[79] Exodus 34:35.

What a change must there be in Lazarus, who once lay among the dogs at the gate of the rich man! What a change has passed over Paul since he lay in the dungeon,—an old man about to be put to death!

Heaven is the city to which all the paths in which good men have walked lead. Is it any wonder that God has made its walls of precious stones, its gates of pearl, and its streets of pure gold?[80] All the hopes, desires, and prayers and praises of the holy family of God centre and terminate in heaven, and it is to be beautiful enough to meet the expectations of all. We cannot, to be sure, tell what eye hath not seen, nor ear heard, nor the heart ever thought of;[81] but we can see that a world where there has been no sin, no clouds, no graves, and no death, and which is intended to be the best of all God's works, must be beautiful. The waters which come leaping down our mountain-sides we call sweet and clear; the air which rocks our trees we call pure; the flowers which grow in our gardens we call beautiful; the fruits which hang on our trees we call pleasant; and the buildings which men can rear we call splendid; but God thinks he can spare all these, and burn them up, and yet have enough left in heaven to make all his friends contented and happy forever! These who have died in the Lord are there. I know that the gray-headed old man is there, and the praying mother is there, and the brother who loved Christ in his youth is there, and the sister who gave her heart to God in her early days is there, and I know that the little child is there, perfecting the praise of God. There the Christian has become an angel, and there the babe has become a cherub, and yet I cannot describe heaven. I cannot begin to describe that.

Is heaven *a place,* or a kind of shadowy land? I reply, it is a place, as much so as this world is a place. Enoch is

---

[80] Revelation 21:15-21.
[81] Isaiah 64:4; 1 Corinthians 2:9.

there, who went to heaven without dying. So is Elijah, who was carried to heaven in a chariot of fire. So is Jesus Christ, and the saints who arose with him at his resurrection. They will have hands and feet and eyes, as we now have, and the world in which they live must be a real place. Over it will hang a fairer sky, purer air, more beautiful light, and all around will be spread new and beautiful sights. Who but God could create such a world! O, it will be every way worthy of him!

And now, my dear children, will you not desire to live so as to go to this heaven when you leave this world? Do you wish that you may there meet the angels and the great and the good who have left this world? Ah! if you may but do that, you will find all the heart can desire, to be your portion for ever. In order to do that, you must remember now your Creator in the days of your youth.[82] Seek the Lord while he may be found; call upon him while he is near.[83] Make God your Father by obeying him, loving and trusting in his Son, Jesus Christ, and then this Father will take you to his beautiful home, to dwell with him for ever and ever. Amen.

THE END

---

[82] Ecclesiastes 12:1.
[83] Read Isaiah 55:6,7.

Other Related Titles from Solid Ground

Mothers of the Wise and Good by Jabez Burns is a new updated edition of the classic book that has strengthened the hands of thousands of women all over the world. High praise from Elisabeth Elliot, Susan Hunt and others.

The Mother at Home: *Raising Your Children in the Fear of the Lord* by John S.C. Abbott. This is the companion volume to *The Child at Home*. This book is deeply convicting and yet, at the same time, greatly encouraging and comforting. Gold dust is upon every page.

The Child at Home: *Living to Please God and Your Parents* by John S.C. Abbott. This is the companion volume to *The Mother at Home*. The response to that book was so encouraging Abbott went to work immediately upon this sequel. We have received numerous endorsements for this book that has been buried a century.

Old Paths for Little Feet by Carol Brandt is a new book from a mother and grandmother who lives in Florida. Mrs. Brandt leads women by the hand in seeking to encourage them to bring their children back to the *"old paths wherein is the good way and walk therein, and ye shall find rest for your souls."* (Jeremiah 6:16)

Little Pillows and Morning Bells by Frances Ridley Havergal
This is one of the finest books to read with young children at the close and the start of every day. Miss Havergal loved children and wrote in such a way that enabled them to grasp difficult concepts by use of familiar images and examples. A heart-warming little volume.

The Pastor's Daughter: *The Way of Salvation Explained to a Young Inquirer by Rev. Edward Payson* by Louisa Payson Hopkins This volume grants us a rare glimpse into the household of the Payson family of Portland, Maine in the early 1800's, as Edward Payson's oldest daughter recalls the patient and loving way her father led her to true conversion over a period of more than 10 years, from 4-14.

Stepping Heavenward by Elizabeth Payson Prentiss
This volume has touched and changed the lives of hundreds of thousands of women all over the world since the day it was first published in 1869. It is a favorite of such ladies as Martha Peace, Elisabeth Elliot, Susan Hunt, Joni Eareskson Tada, Kay Arthur and many, many more.

The Young Lady's Guide: *to the Harmonious Development of Christian Character* by Harvey Newcomb. One pastor has said, *"It should be read, studied, prayed over, and put into practice by parents, young ladies, and—yes—even young men! It should be in every home, and in the library of every young lady. It is a 'companion' book for a lifetime."* We could not agree more!

Call us Toll Free at **1-877-666-9469**

Other SGCB Classic Reprints

Solid Ground Christian Books is honored to present the following titles, many for the first time in more than a century:

COLLECTED WORKS of James Henley Thornwell (4 vols.)

CALVINISM IN HISTORY *by Nathaniel S. McFetridge*

OPENING SCRIPTURE: *Hermeneutical Manual by Patrick Fairbairn*

THE ASSURANCE OF FAITH *by Louis Berkhof*

THE PASTOR IN THE SICK ROOM *by John D. Wells*

THE BUNYAN OF BROOKLYN: *Life & Sermons of I.S. Spencer*

THE NATIONAL PREACHER: S*ermons from 2nd Great Awakening*

FIRST THINGS: F*irst Lessons God Taught Mankind* Gardiner Spring

BIBLICAL & THEOLOGICAL STUDIES *by 1912 Faculty of Princeton*

THE POWER OF GOD UNTO SALVATION *by B.B. Warfield*

THE LORD OF GLORY *by B.B. Warfield*

A GENTLEMAN & A SCHOLAR: *Memoir of J.P. Boyce by J. Broadus*

SERMONS TO THE NATURAL MAN *by W.G.T. Shedd*

SERMONS TO THE SPIRITUAL MAN *by W.G.T. Shedd*

HOMILETICS AND PASTORAL THEOLOGY *by W.G.T. Shedd*

A PASTOR'S SKETCHES 1 & 2 *by Ichabod S. Spencer*

THE PREACHER AND HIS MODELS *by James Stalker*

IMAGO CHRISTI *by James Stalker*

A HISTORY OF PREACHING *by Edwin C. Dargan*

LECTURES ON THE HISTORY OF PREACHING *by J. A. Broadus*

THE SCOTTISH PULPIT *by William Taylor*

THE SHORTER CATECHISM ILLUSTRATED *by John Whitecross*

THE CHURCH MEMBER'S GUIDE *by John Angell James*

THE SUNDAY SCHOOL TEACHER'S GUIDE *by John A. James*

CHRIST IN SONG: *Hymns of Immanuel from All Ages by Philip Schaff*

COME YE APART: *Daily Words from the Four Gospels by J.R. Miller*

DEVOTIONAL LIFE OF THE S.S. TEACHER *by J.R. Miller*

Call us Toll Free at 1-877-666-9469
Send us an e-mail at sgcb@charter.net
Visit us on line at solid-ground-books.com

Uncovering Buried Treasure to the Glory of God

p. 12 (reading)
" (thinking)
13 (feeling)
'14 (doing / conscience)

Lightning Source UK Ltd.
Milton Keynes UK

176209UK00001B/217/A